Stewardship Economy   5

efficient, fair taxes
and the role of the state

Julian Pratt

Published by

Lulu.com

Editorial note

This book brings together previously unpublished material which
Julian worked on alongside the summary book, *Stewardship
Economy 1: private property without private ownership*. With the
other five books in the series, it provides the additional material
that lies behind the proposals and assertions made in book 1.
Unfortunately, aspects of this work are unfinished, some of the
examples provided are out of date, there is some repetition of text
and some references (bibliography in book 7) are not available. I
hope you, the reader, will excuse this and will find the work as a
whole thought-provoking and topical.

Rosemary Field

September 2021

ISBN 978-1-4717-0178-8

Contents

Books in the series

Stewardship Economy 1: private property without private ownership is the first book and provides an overall summary of the main ideas.

Stewardship Economy 2: Valuing land and managing transition sets out in some detail how to establish the market rent of land and how to make the transition from an ownership to a stewardship economy. It also considers how the revenue from stewardship fees might be distributed.

Stewardship Economy 3: Land, environment and climate (this book) explores how a stewardship economy would transform the way we use land, provide housing and develop our cities. It goes on to consider how stewardship would help address pressing environmental and climate concerns.

Stewardship Economy 4: The economy, wealth and universal income focuses on the impact of stewardship on the national and global economy, how the distribution of wealth would be changed and the impact of a Universal Income.

Stewardship Economy 5: efficient, fair taxes and the role of the state (this book) describes the some of the adverse effects of our current system of taxation and considers the role of the state in a stewardship economy. It also explains some basic economic principles and terms.

Stewardship Economy 6: property rights describes the systems of property rights in our current economic system, their history and how property rights could be more fair and efficient in a stewardship economy.

Stewardship Economy 7: some economics explained, economic terms and bibliography. This book provides an introduction to some key economic concepts for the non-specialist and lists the references, as far as they are available.

Introduction

This book sets out to demonstrate how a stewardship economy is more economically efficient than an economy based on ownership. Land is used more efficiently, enabling profitable production close to the margin of production. Conventional taxes are inefficient as they generate a deadweight loss, while stewardship fees do not. There are also efficiencies in collection of stewardship fees.

Chapter 1 explores the nature of rent. Rent arises because there is competition for land, which is effectively fixed in quantity. Rent is a surplus above and beyond the amount needed to keep labour and capital in production on a marginal site. Chapter 2 describes how conventional forms of taxation have harmful effects on the economy, while a charge or tax on market rents is beneficial. Chapter 3 considers efficiency of taxes: economic efficiency, efficiency of collection and efficient use of marginal land. Chapter 4 looks at fairness of taxation in ownership and stewardship economies.

Part II considers the role of the state in a stewardship economy. Chapter 6 looks at the impact of state funding of transport infrastructure and Chapter 7 explores briefly their role in other public services.

Part I   Efficiency and Fairness of Taxes

Chapter 1   Rent is a surplus

Rent arises because land is scarce

If there was plenty of desirable land, available for people simply to claim, there would be nothing to pay for its use. As desirable land is scarce, we expect to have to pay rent to whoever controls this use. Adam Smith (1723-1790) (1776 Vol I Book I Chapter XI: 214) was quite clear that a landlord endeavours set the rent at such a level as to leave his tenants with no greater share of the produce than they need to pay their costs and provide an ordinary level of profit.

David Ricardo (1772 –1823) distinguished between two sorts of commodities. Some, such as manufactured goods, have a price-elastic supply and when demand increases, the potential revenue stream calls more labour and capital into production. Others, such as land, have a price-inelastic supply that is fixed – no more can be brought into production by the prospect of the potential revenue. Ricardo stated that useful commodities:

'derive their exchangeable value from two sources: from their scarcity, and from the quantity of labour required to obtain them.

There are some commodities, the value of which is determined by their scarcity alone. No labour can increase the quantity of such goods, and therefore their value cannot be lowered by an increased supply. Some rare statues and pictures, scarce books and coins, wines of a peculiar quality, which can be made only from grapes grown on a particular soil, of which there is a very limited quantity, are all of this description. Their value is wholly independent of the quantity of labour originally necessary to produce them and varies with the varying wealth and inclinations of those who are desirous to possess them.

These commodities, however, form a very small part of the mass of commodities daily exchanged in the market. By far the greatest part of these goods which are the objects of desire, are procured by labour; and they may be multiplied, not in one country alone, but in many, almost without any assignable limit, if we are disposed to bestow the labour necessary to obtain them (David Ricardo 1817 Chapter I :2).'

As land and natural resources cannot be created, they are relatively price-inelastic, and their value is determined by this scarcity. Ricardo uses the term 'rent' to describe the return to the landowner for the use of the land. Although he stressed the contribution of the 'original and indestructible powers of the soil' to the productive capacity of the land, he was writing primarily about the return to a particular location (David Ricardo 1817 Chapter II:49).

'On the first settling of a country, in which there is an abundance of rich and fertile land, a very small proportion of which is required to be cultivated for the support of the actual population, or indeed can be cultivated with the capital which the population can command, there will be no rent; for no one would pay for the use of land, when there was an abundant quantity not yet appropriated, and therefore at the disposal of whosoever might choose to cultivate it....

'If all land had the same properties, if it were boundless in quantity, and uniform in quality, no charge could be made for its use, unless where it possessed peculiar advantages of situation. It is only, then, because land is of different qualities with respect to its productive powers [in later editions not unlimited in quantity and uniform in quality], and because in the progress of population, land of an inferior quality, or less advantageously situated, is called into cultivation, that rent is ever paid for the use of it. When in the progress of society, land of the second degree of fertility is taken into cultivation, rent immediately commences on that of the first quality, and the amount of that rent will depend on the difference in the quality of these two portions of land.

'When land of the third quality is taken into cultivation, rent immediately commences on the second, and it is regulated as before, by the difference in their productive powers. At the same time, the rent of the first quality will rise, for that must always be above the rent of the second by the difference between the produce which they yield with a given quantity of capital and labour. With every step in the progress of population, which shall oblige a country to have recourse to land of a worse quality, to enable it to raise its supply of food, rent, on all the more fertile land, will rise (David Ricardo 1817 Chapter II:52).'

Ricardo focused his attention on agricultural rents, partly because of their simplicity (avoiding the complication of buildings attached to the land) but mainly because of the overwhelming importance of the agricultural sector in the economy of the day. Rent may arise on any land or natural resources including, for example, the radio spectrum.

Even where the person owning the land and the person using the land are one and the same, the land still has an imputed or notional market rent that would be revealed if it was exposed to the market.

In the UK in 1990, 90 per cent of the value of the surface of the land was used for industry, commerce, housing and public services; and less than 10 per cent for agriculture land and forest (Ronald Banks 1989:39). The following example therefore transposes one of Ricardo's examples to a retail setting.

Think of three shops in a city - No. 1 at a prime location at the city centre, No. 2 located on a street of secondary importance and No. 3 located away from the usual shopping areas. Because they are more or less likely to attract custom, application of the same amount of capital (including buildings) and labour to these shops may be expected to generate different levels of income. Suppose that they can return a weekly income of £1,000, £900 and £800 respectively. (These figures reflect the potential of the site in the highest and best use that anyone is willing to put it to, not in its current actual use). Wages will be broadly similar in shops throughout the city, and each of the businesses will have to pay similar rates of interest on the capital they have borrowed - but the owner of the land will be able to demand a higher rent for the most profitable site. If each of the shops has a total weekly expenditure (on labour, capital, stock and running expenses) of £800, then shop No. 3 is described as being at the margin of production – it is a marginal site. On this site the landlord will be able to charge no rent at all (if he did, the shop would have to cease trading) while shop No. 2 will have a weekly market rent of £100 and shop No. 1 a weekly market rent of £200 (after David Ricardo 1817 Chapter II:55).

The rent payable on a plot of land is equal to the difference between the wealth created at that location and the wealth created by the same inputs at the least productive site on which anyone would choose to engage in production (the margin of production). Although this example relies on the existence of a marginal site for comparison purposes, Ricardo also demonstrated that rent can arise when the employment of additional labour or capital produces diminishing returns at the same site (David Ricardo 1817 Chapter II).

Rent is a surplus

Workers need to be paid; they have to live and eat and be housed. Capital also needs to be rewarded – for risk, for the cost of producing machinery and its deterioration, and to match the return available on risk-free investments such as government bonds. But land just exists, it does not need a financial reward to continue to exist. The payment of rent is not needed to bring land into production, and rent is a surplus.

One of David Ricardo's great insights was that, in general, people supplying labour and capital are prepared to take part in production on good land and on bad for the same return (wages and interest). Rent is the surplus above and beyond the return needed to keep labour and capital in production. It arises because there is competition for an asset (high quality land) whose supply is effectively fixed (price-inelastic).

The economic surplus

Neoclassical economists used the tools of equilibrium analysis to develop a greater understanding of the nature of rent and the economic surplus. Suppose that I go to an auction and see something I want to buy. I will decide the maximum that I am prepared to pay and bid up to that amount – which is what it is 'really' worth to me. If I buy it for exactly that price, I am content with the purchase. If the bidding stops below this level, I feel I have got a bargain.

A consumer will want to make a purchase when its value to her (its utility) is greater than its purchase price. The difference between these two prices, summed across all consumers, is the 'consumer surplus', a measure of the value consumers get from their purchases over and above the amount they pay for them. A producer will want to make a sale when the sale price is greater than the cost of production. The difference between these two prices, summed across all producers, is the 'producer surplus', a measure of the extra revenue that producers get over and above what they need to engage in production. The sum of the producer and consumer surpluses is the 'economic surplus', a measure of the amount the whole economy benefits from production.

When supply is fixed in amount (price-inelastic), as in the case of land, there are no production costs and the whole of the 'producer surplus' is available to the landowner as rent.

This is shown below in Fig 1. You may decide to skip this, and the graphs in the next two chapters – either because the material is already familiar to you or because you don't find graphs helpful. But if it is unfamiliar, and you really want to understand the idea of efficient taxation that is such an important aspect of stewardship, you may want to look at book 7 now which explains this.

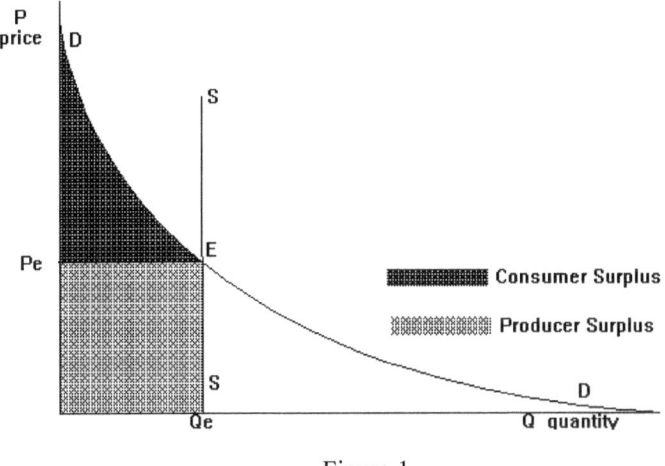

Figure 1.

There has been general agreement for over 200 years that the market rent of land is a surplus above and beyond the return needed to keep labour and capital in production. This is conferred by the advantages of that location over and above a marginal location.

Chapter 2   Taxation reduces market rent

Taxes discourage whatever is being taxed and reduce the economic surplus. The economic surplus is the source of the market rent of land, so taxes reduce rent. This chapter, supplemented if you wish by the annex, explains this step by step. If you think of a stewardship economy and imagine the introduction of a new tax, that tax will not generate any net revenue as the gross revenue it generates will be offset by an equal reduction in rent and so in stewardship fees. Taxes in a stewardship economy are used to change behaviour, not to raise revenue. Conversely, when taxes are removed market rents of all land rise as householders and businesses find themselves with greater disposable income and landowners step in to increase the rent.

When people look at the market rent of the UK as an ownership economy and question whether stewardship fees could provide the government with sufficient revenue, they may be forgetting that the revenue will stimulate the economy, by reducing orthodox taxes, distribution of a Universal Income or as government spending, and resulting in increase in rents.

Ideally, a Land Value Tax should always be introduced in a revenue-neutral way, accompanied by a reduction in other taxes. This creates a virtuous cycle in which the market rent of land net of Land Value Tax remains more- or-less constant.

Taxation in an ownership economy

A closed economy is sometimes described using the circular flow model, which clarifies the way that different forms of taxation affect the economy as a whole. The figure below ignores savings and investment, imports and exports:

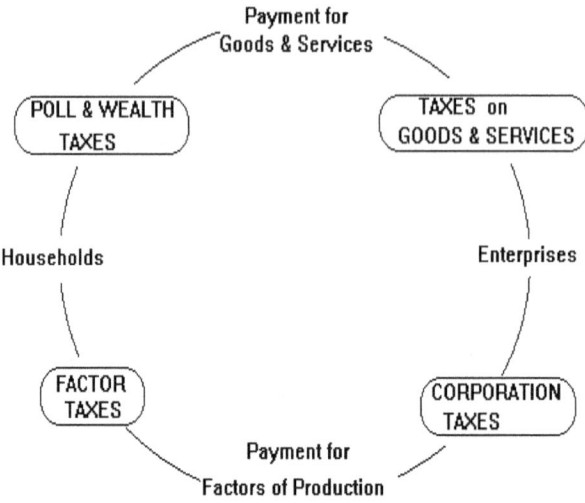

Figure 2.

Money circulating in the economy can be extracted by taxation of any stage of the flow. Money removed by taxation from one arm will not be available to be taxed from another arm. Conversely, if one tax is reduced the money may be available for taxation elsewhere in the circular flow.

Businesses pay **Corporation Taxes** on their profits. These either reduce the capital available for reinvestment in the enterprise or reduce the payment to the factors of production – land, labour and capital. **Factor Taxes** are levied on all forms of income - rent, wages and interest. These taxes reduce the income of landowners, workers and owners of capital and so reduce household income.

It is unusual for any tax to fall solely on one factor of production. Income Tax falls on all three factors of production – on income from work (wages), on income from land ownership (rent) and on income from investment in capital (interest). Property taxes such as local authority rates or council tax are a tax on both buildings (capital) and the land on which they stand. National Insurance contributions are a tax on labour. An increase in the value of capital or of land is a capitalisation of future expected increases in interest or rent and may be taxed by Capital Gains Taxes.

Poll & Wealth Taxes are taxes on individuals and on owning wealth (capital or land). Their impact is to reduce the amount of goods and services that households can buy. Wealth taxes include taxes on wealth owned and on gifts of wealth from one individual to another (capital transfer taxes), including bequests (Inheritance Tax). These taxes reduce the wealth of individuals.

Taxes on Goods & Services include excise duties, sales taxes and VAT. These taxes are sometimes known as 'indirect taxes' although this term also includes import tariffs and property taxes. These taxes reduce the income of enterprises.

Most taxes reduce the economic surplus

It is possible to apply taxes at any point in the circular flow; but if one tax takes away some of the economic surplus created by enterprise, that part of the surplus is no longer available elsewhere in the circular flow to be captured by a different form of tax.

At the marginal site, production generates just enough income to pay for the labour and capital used. If tax (whether this be Income Tax, VAT, Corporation Tax, National Insurance or even a tax on land) is levied at the marginal site production will cease. It is only at sites above the margin that a tax can be levied – sites on which rent arises. If a tax is levied, the rent (net of tax) will fall. All taxes apart from poll tax and a tax on land reduce the economic surplus, as described in the annex and shown below (Figure 3 next page). A tax on wealth initially has no impact on the economic surplus as the wealth has already been created, but, as expectations grow that wealth will be taxed, it comes to operate as a tax on production.

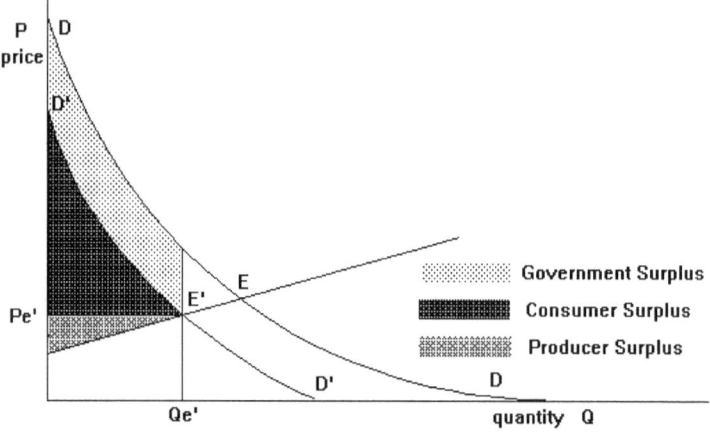

Figure 3.

Removing taxes causes market rents to rise

If a tax is reduced or removed then the economic surplus increases and market rents rise.

Tax havens

There are many states and jurisdictions that levy little or no tax on income or business, places like Jersey and Monaco. These are highly desirable locations for people who would be high taxpayers in countries with more conventional tax regimes, and therefore the value of land there is high. If taxes were introduced, the value of the land would fall. This is a rather extreme example of the general principle – that all forms of taxation reduce the market rent of land.

Enterprise zones

In the USA local property taxes (on land and buildings) may be waived to attract developers. Thatcher borrowed this idea for her 'Enterprise Zones' in the UK in 1981. These were intended to increase enterprise in areas of high unemployment by allowing significant freedom from planning controls, granting exemption from business rates and Development Land Tax for 10 years, and providing grants and tax allowances for capital expenditure on industrial and commercial buildings. In these zones rents and sale prices rose, starting on Budget day when the scheme was announced and initially in the areas landlords thought might be designated as Enterprise Zones (Fred Harrison 1983:265). Rising rents neutralised any benefit to the enterprises that used the sites, as confirmed ten years later by the Second Interim Evaluation of Enterprise Zones in 1995:

'The capital allowance concession increases the rate of return to developers and again tends to feed through into higher land values. The rates concession represents a direct saving to tenants (and owner occupiers) but there is evidence that it is largely offset by higher market rents, which in turn feed through into capital and land values' (Department of the Environment 1988:40).

It was landowners who benefited, while local and central government suffered a loss of tax revenue and enterprises were relatively unaffected.

Supply-side policies

When government embarks on supply-side fiscal policies such as cutting taxes on labour and capital to stimulate employment and investment, the impact is limited because the increased income of firms leaks into rising property prices (George Gilder 1981 via Banks 1989:150 - but Gilder may be seen as an apologist for elitism).

Impact on market rents

The amount of rent that a tenant is willing to pay for a site depends on their estimate of the profitability or utility of the site. What matters to them is the total amount of rent and any tax they need to pay – an insight known as the 'equation theory' (Hector Wilks 1984:187 sect 8.13). If taxes are reduced, rents will rise. The extent to which market rents rise when taxes are reduced depends on the extent to which the demand for land can be substituted by other goods, in which case market rents will rise by less than the amount by which the tax is reduced. Though rents might increase by more than the amount of tax removed if this leads to an increase in the economic surplus.

Taxes in a stewardship economy generate no net revenue

In an established stewardship economy introducing orthodox taxes will produce a fall market rents and so in stewardship fees. The revenue from the tax may not be enough to compensate for the fall in stewardship fees (deadweight loss) so total revenues (tax + stewardship fees) are likely to fall.

It possible to discuss the benefits and disbenefits of particular taxes without linking them to revenue generation and this is particularly important for taxes and charges that are intended to influence behaviour, such as the emission of greenhouse gases or the use of water. These cost an average consumer almost nothing in a stewardship economy if they are a steward of land, because any tax will be offset by an automatic fall in market rents and so in stewardship fees. But tax still influences behaviour because most consumers are not average and the tax falls more heavily on those who consume more than an equal share. Those who consume less than an equal share receive a net income as their tax costs are outweighed by the fall in their stewardship fees.

In the longer term a well-designed tax or charge can increase per capita GDP. Charges for greenhouse gas emissions are intended to prevent ecological collapse, and if they succeed they will have led to far higher levels of income than if that collapse occurs. Similarly, a tax on alcohol causes people who drink to pay something more like the true cost of these activities to society. This may result in a population that is healthier, has lower health care costs and greater productivity, and so has a higher level of GDP per capita.

Chapter 3 Efficiency of taxes

Which taxes promote economic efficiency? And which can be collected most efficiently? Which stimulate the efficient use of marginal land? And which promote efficient markets, including an efficient land market?

Stewardship fees are intended to provide an answer to the question 'who shall have exclusive use of a particular plot of land, or other aspect of the natural world?' The rationale for stewardship fees is independent of the need for taxation, which is why they are fees not taxes. Stewardship fees can be used to fund transfer payments to individuals, such as a Universal Income, or to provide revenue for the state to support the common good. In ownership economies the state currently raises taxes for these two purposes, so a comparison between stewardship fees and taxation is inevitable. Adam Smith (1776 Volume III Book V Chapter II:208) described four maxims by which to judge taxes which address their efficiency, certainty and convenience and fairness. Efficiency here includes both economic efficiency and efficiency of collection. Conventional taxes are inefficient, particularly because they cause a deadweight loss.

Economic efficiency

The efficiency of a tax is equal to the amount of revenue it delivers for the government divided by the sum of this revenue and the deadweight loss.

Avoiding the deadweight loss of taxes

The key issue by which the efficiency of a tax should be judged is its effect on the overall level of economic activity. Stewardship fees prevent land speculation, ensure that land is used efficiently, and money is invested in productive assets instead of acquiring land and the natural world. But the most familiar argument in favour of stewardship is that it makes it possible to remove conventional taxes, which are inefficient because they create a deadweight loss.

Ownership economy

Taxes discourage whatever is being taxed. This may be the intention of a tax, such as those applied to alcohol, tobacco, fossil fuel or plastic bags. Or its effects may be unintended. Because VAT is charged on repairs and refurbishments of people's homes, while new construction is free from VAT, the tax discourages refurbishment and encourages both demolition of viable buildings and construction on greenfield sites.

Taxation distorts the way the whole economy works. Taxing savings reduces the pool of resources that is available for investment and encourages current consumption. Taxing labour promotes capital-intensive production, taxing capital encourages labour-intensive activity. If one country imposes high levels of taxation on labour, they risk driving jobs away as they become less competitive. High levels of taxation on goods stimulate smuggling from countries where taxes are lower. Firms that can make a profit in a tax-free environment find it harder to do so when taxes are levied, and this discourages entrepreneurship.

All taxes on income, profits, sales and so on cause the price that a buyer pays to be greater than the price that the seller receives, and if this is greater than the potential gain from the transaction it may be enough to prevent that transaction from taking place.

Even where taxation reduces supply and demand by only a small amount, it reduces overall economic activity – the 'lost surplus' or 'deadweight loss of taxation' (Figure 4 next page).

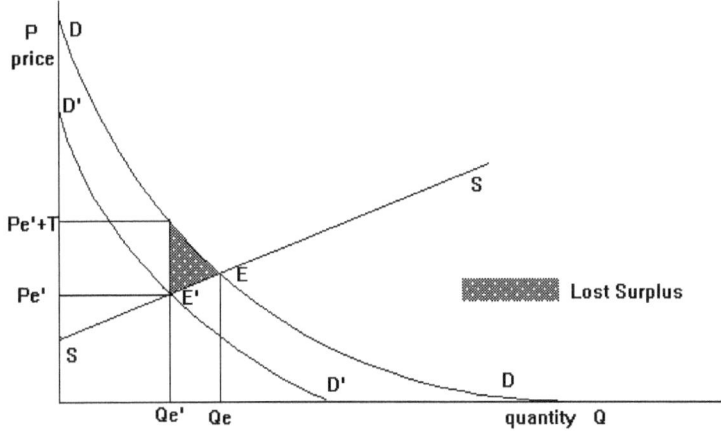

Figure 4. (see book 7 for explanation)

The deadweight loss is the amount of lost economic activity for each £1 of taxes raised. Geographically it has its most devastating impact at the margin of production – at those locations where business is only just hanging on – and so has a disproportionate impact on disadvantaged communities.

Most estimates of the deadweight loss of taxes refer to the marginal loss, which is the figure that is needed when considering marginal changes in taxation in an ownership economy. When considering the impact of a wholesale change from ownership to stewardship, the relevant figure is the total annual deadweight loss.

Estimates of the deadweight loss depend on the underlying model of the economy that is used; and on the estimates of elasticity, for example the elasticity of savings and of the supply of labour, that are made. Several estimates of the deadweight loss are given below, which suggest that a figure of 20-30 per cent of taxes raised (range 15 – 50) is a reasonable estimate.

❑ A general equilibrium model of the US economy has been used to estimate the total deadweight loss of all taxes, when compared with a non-distortionary lump-sum tax, at 13-24 per cent of the tax revenue (Charles Ballard et al 1985b:125).

❑ Other models suggest values between 18 per cent (Dale Jorgenson and Kun-Young Yun 1991:488) and 30 per cent (Martin Feldstein 1999:674).

- 20 to 50 per cent (Auerbach & Feldstein 2002) from empirical studies]
- Nicolaus Tideman and Florenz Plassman (1998:147) use a general equilibrium model of the G7 economies to model the impact of a change from current taxes to a Land Value Tax (which has no deadweight loss) (Book 7). This model assumes that the new tax will increase the efficiency of land use, which increases the impact of the change, though this is partially offset by the retention of a small income tax after the change. They found that in the USA taxes in 1993 caused a loss of around $6,000 in per capita NDP. In the UK taxes in 1993, imposed at a higher rate than in the USA, caused a loss of around £12,000 in per capita NDP. Taxation in 1993 meant that the economy was functioning at only 77 per cent of its potential in the USA and 55 per cent of its potential in the UK. Ronald Banks, who has campaigned to get the National Audit Office to estimate the deadweight loss of taxes (1989) estimates that it amounts in the UK to £14,500 per person per year.
- The UK Treasury does not make an independent estimate of the deadweight loss of taxes, total or marginal (Fred Harrison 2006:44), but it uses a value for the lost surplus, which it calls the Social Opportunity Cost of Exchequer Funds (SOCEF), of 30 per cent (30p for each £1 raised). (Department for Transport 2009)

Even a 20 per cent deadweight loss imposes a heavy burden on the economy. In 2003–2004, the total UK tax take was £399 billion, of which about 80 per cent (£320 billion) fell on work and enterprise. This means that, taking an estimate of the total burden of 20 per cent, the annual deadweight loss of these taxes is over £80 billion.

None of this is to be taken as an argument against taxation and government spending in an ownership economy. Most government spending brings benefits that outweigh the deadweight loss of the associated taxes. There is no evidence that high levels of taxation lead to low rates of GDP growth (Polly Toynbee 2008:216). If we want the benefits of government expenditure, in an ownership economy we need to put up with the deadweight loss.

Economic growth is not necessarily desirable, given the environmental damage it currently causes and the way of life it engenders. But in an ownership economy economic growth is the aim of government policy and it would be better to be in a position to choose zero growth than to be forced into it.

Stewardship economy

Taxes levied on things that are fixed in supply, such as land, are efficient in that they create no lost surplus and impose no deadweight loss (Figure 5.). They do not distort the amount of land made available or put to use. They do not reduce production, consumption, prosperity or GDP. They are called Ramsey taxes, after the economist Frank Ramsey.

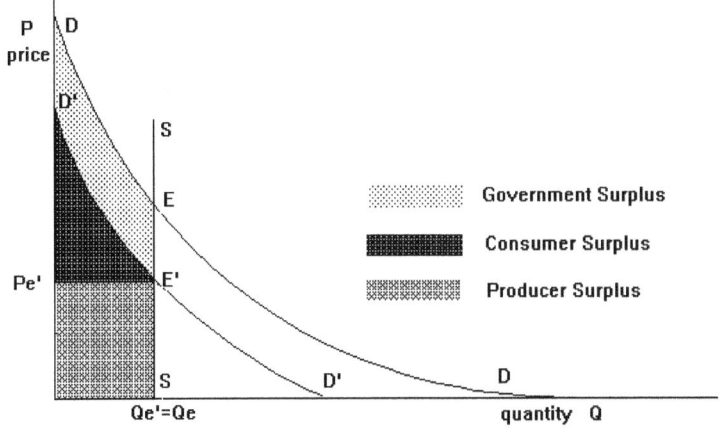

Figure 5.

This lack of a deadweight loss, along with the release of underused land to those who need it, is the central pragmatic reason for advocating stewardship.

Both ground-rents and the ordinary rent of land are a species of revenue which the owner, in many cases, enjoys without any care or attention of his own. Though a part of this revenue should be taken from him in order to defray the expenses of the state, no discouragement will thereby be given to any form of industry. The annual produce of the land and labour of the society, the real wealth and revenue of the great one of the people, might be the same after such a tax as before. Ground-rents, and the ordinary rent of land, are therefore, perhaps, the species of revenue which can best bear to have a peculiar tax imposed upon them (Adam Smith 1776 Volume III Chapter V: 239*).*

Transition from ownership to stewardship creates a 'tax shift' away from taxing things that we want to encourage, like labour and profits, and on to land.

If UK government revenue were funded from stewardship fees rather than from conventional taxation, we would expect that economic activity would be around £80 billion per year higher – more than £1300 for every man, woman and child in the UK.

A stewardship economy could be entirely free from the deadweight loss of taxes because stewardship fees can provide all the revenue that the government needs, indeed all the revenue that it is possible to collect. If taxes on alcohol and tobacco are imposed in a stewardship economy this is because they are intended to act as a deterrent to consumption, not because they are a source of revenue. The deadweight loss they create is desirable.

The only other sort of tax that is free from a deadweight loss is the poll tax, which although efficient is massively unfair and regressive, falling equally on everyone.

Preventing speculation

A charge on the market rent of land has the beneficial effect of reducing the gains to be had from holding land. Stewardship fees equal to 100 per cent of market rent reduce the market value of land to zero, and even the transition mechanism holds its market value constant. This means that as long as the valuations really are kept up to date there are no gains to be had from speculating in land.

Land used more intensively-

Speculators are the group of people who are most optimistic that market rents and market values of land will rise (by more than the opportunity cost of leaving it idle), and so they are least likely to invest in productive improvements (as well as being unable to do so as they may already have paid too much for the land). Speculation leads to underuse of land, which is generally inefficient (unless it really would be more productive to delay development so that the land remains unencumbered by relatively low-rent developments).

Land is used in a way which is more productive in a stewardship economy and there is less investment in land destined to be used unproductively, so stewardship ensures that there is more land available for productive use.

Making the best use of land

Stewardship does more than remove any incentive to speculate in land, it counteracts the speculative tinge that causes people in an ownership economy to hold just a bit more land, or more valuable land, than they really need. In a stewardship economy people only occupy land when they have a good reason to do so and are prepared to pay the stewardship fees. A stewardship economy therefore reduces the artificial scarcity in land caused by speculation and makes more land readily available for productive use.

Efficient investment

Speculation in ownership economies diverts investment from production to land so productive investment is greater in a stewardship economy. Taxes on savings are removed. Investment is directed at businesses with sound business plans, not businesses with property to offer as collateral.

Efficiency of collection

The efficiency of tax collection is the ratio of the tax recovered to the tax that should be available for collection (before the costs of collection and the tax lost through avoidance and evasion).

Cheap and easy to collect

'Every tax ought to be so contrived as both to take out and to keep out of the pockets of the people as little as possible over and above what it brings into the public treasury of the state (Adam Smith Volume III Book V Chapter II:209).'

Adam Smith was concerned not just by the way in which taxes introduce market inefficiencies but with the costs incurred in assessing and collecting the tax. Any estimate of the cost of collecting taxes must include not just the cost to the state but the costs to individuals, businesses and their accountants in playing their part. Smith's concerns went beyond simply time and cost; he opposed the exposure of taxpayers to 'frequent visits and odious examinations of tax-gatherers', whom he considered to be responsible for 'much unnecessary trouble, vexation and oppression'.

Conventional taxes

The costs to the government of collecting conventional taxes range from 0.6 per cent (National Insurance) to 1.4 per cent (Income Tax, Inheritance Tax). (Inland Revenue via Economist 28/8/04 p28). No figures are generally available in the UK for the costs to individuals and companies, but it would be surprising if the costs did not exceed 0.5 – 1.0 per cent of the revenue raised in the case of taxes like Income Tax, Corporation Tax and VAT.

In the USA the cost of tax collection was estimated to be at least $100 billion a year in 1995 (Economist 13/1/96:50). In addition, Americans spend 3.5 billion hours a year doing their taxes, about 26 hours per household, and spend about $140 billion on professional help related to tax liability (Economist 15/4/06).

Stewardship fees

The cost of setting up a land register would be significant but not excessive. A significant proportion of the set-up costs have already been incurred in high-consumption economies, where there is experience of both national databases of ownership (e.g., Land Registries), and local databases held for taxation purposes (e.g., council tax). These systems have not generally, however, included separate valuations of the land and the improvements. Both the total value of the property and the value of the improvements need to be established at set-up, and the initial costs may amount to 1–10 per cent of annual tax revenues as a one-off.

Complying with transition to stewardship will involve cost and vexation to landowners at the start-up. At this time anyone owning land or natural resources will need to make it available for a visit by a valuer. There will be no further cost or vexation unless they wish to appeal against this initial valuation.

There will be significant but not excessive costs to the Land Stewardship Trust in administering the land register, revaluing the improvements and updating the stewardship fees. In Denmark, where land was valued annually for tax purposes, the cost of valuations and collecting the tax was less than 2 per cent of the revenue raised (Ronald Banks 1989:176 or 1998:125). These costs will be met from the general income from stewardship fees, not from charges to individual stewards. There will be no further cost or vexation to stewards unless they improve or pollute their site, or they wish to appeal.

The total cost of tax-gathering, and the intrusion on taxpayers, would be substantially less in a stewardship economy than in an ownership economy with its multitude of taxes all requiring their own assessment and collection mechanisms.

Difficult to avoid and evade

Tax evasion is the use of illegal means to reduce an individual's or company's tax liability, usually by making a false declaration of income or expenditure. Adam Smith feared that taxpayers would be tempted to evade taxes, for example by smuggling, and then be ruined by the penalties for doing so. Tax compliance is compliance with the spirit of the law and attempting to pay the right amount of tax. Tax avoidance is the area in between evasion and compliance – behaviours that are not illegal but are conscious attempts to get round the law. These include transferring assets to a person or entity that pays less tax, changing employment income into investment income and declaring profits in a tax haven that have been earned elsewhere (Richard Murphy 2008:16).

One reason that conventional taxes are inefficient to collect is the time and energy that goes into tax avoidance. This includes the professional costs of accountants, lawyers and independent financial advisers who advise on legal ways to minimise and avoid taxes, as well as the work of civil servants to anticipate and react to these schemes.

Conventional taxes

Conventional taxes face problems of avoidance due both to the shift of commercial activities to low-tax environments and uncertainty about the country in which a tax should be levied. They are also prone to evasion.

Firms and people can exploit differences between countries and relocate to favourable tax regimes. As countries compete to retain production within their borders they may embark on a 'race to the bottom' as they successively cut tax rates. The 30 market-based economies of the Organisation for Economic Co-operation and Development cut their rates of Corporation Tax by 7 percentage points between 1996 and 2003, with Ireland cutting it by 23 percentage points. A 'race to the bottom' causes tax revenues to fall and production to shift to low-tax countries.

It can be difficult and complicated to know in which country a tax should be levied – for example for cross-border internet purchases or for taxes paid by multinational corporations. These uncertainties lead to errors and open the door to avoidance and evasion.

Liability for tax may depend on where the income stream arises or where consumption take place. On the internet it becomes difficult to locate these geographically. To take one example, if a consumer in Europe buys a product from a local subsidiary of an American firm or orders it directly from America by post, they pay European tax rates. If they order or download the same product over the internet they are liable to tax in America.

The 'hidden economy' is economic activity that is hidden from the authorities, perhaps to avoid regulation or taxation. It is difficult to estimate the size of this hidden economy, but it is thought that nearly 20 per cent of all tax revenues in OECD countries are evaded, 40 per cent in low-consumption countries and 60 per cent in Zimbabwe (Economist 13/5/06:92). Income tax and VAT are commonly avoided and evaded.

In the UK about £25 billion is lost to the government each year from legal tax avoidance (Richard Murphy 2008:29) – enough to increase the basic state pension by 20 per cent *and* to raise the threshold for the higher rate of tax by £10,000 per year, for example.

Tax avoidance and evasion is of increasing importance with the globalisation of the economy and the development of information technology. Production, labour and savings are all increasingly mobile, and globalisation poses challenges to the taxation policies of nation-states. The expansion of the internet makes it increasingly difficult to keep track of, and tax, transfers of goods and services across boundaries. This will only increase if there is a proliferation of alternative cryptocurrencies.

Sixty per cent of all international trade takes place within multinational firms, and these organisations may shift their tax burden by skilful transfer pricing between national subsidiaries, paying low prices for components or services produced in a high-tax environment, for example. A study conducted by the Center for Banking and Financial Institutions at Florida International University in Miami, Florida, and reported to the US senate, claimed that multinationals had evaded up to $45 billion in 2000 – in one case by selling toothbrushes between subsidiaries for more than $5000 dollars each (reported in Multinational Monitor 2001 https://www.proquest.com/openview/84f31b6d7647c48a67013ebfa570af39/1?pq-origsite=gscholar&cbl=48578)

Even in America, with its relatively low-tax regime and therefore low incentives for tax evasion, about 15 per cent of personal income is thought to be undeclared. Almost all the big corporate scandals of recent years have included the evasion of tax, often with the support of accountancy firms. In the UK about £11.3 billion was estimated to have been lost to VAT fraud in 2004-2005. This evasion ranges from builders' 'cash jobs' to elaborate international 'carousel' fraud. Across Europe the figure was probably about 100 € billion (Economist 13/5/06:95).

Tax revenues lost in this way, and the cost of detecting and prosecuting evasion, are recouped through higher levels of taxation on people who do comply with the demands of taxation. This is both unfair and inefficient.

For all these reasons, governments will need to rely more on taxes on things that are visible and immobile – consumption, low skilled (relatively immobile) workers and land. But transferring taxation to the least well paid is unfair; large international differences between levels of consumption taxes stimulate unproductive cross-border shopping and smuggling of high-value items. The amount of tax that can be raised from consumption and low-paid workers has its limits, leaving only land as an immovable and reliable source of tax revenues.

As it is not possible to hide land and the valuation process is public, it is difficult to imagine how stewardship fees might be evaded. This recognition is not new:

'Domesday Book about which you inquire, is the inescapable companion in the Treasury of the royal seal... The book is metaphorically called by the native English Domesday, i.e., the Day of Judgement. For as the sentence of that strict and terrible last account cannot be eroded by any skilful subterfuge, so when the book is appealed to... its sentence cannot be quashed or set aside with impunity' (Richard Fitz Nigel c 1176).

The Economist, even back in 1997 when it was not known for its advocacy of taxes on land values, concluded a review on 'Disappearing Taxes' in the era of the internet by concluding that landed property is one of the few things that has an unavoidable physical presence, and they raised the question of whether our post-industrial age would have to return to what it described as a pre-industrial tax system (31/5/97:21).

Taxes on land values, like stewardship, may be particularly attractive in countries such as Estonia, where a significant amount of land is owned by foreign nationals, in this case Russian landholdings. Stewardship ensures that the local population benefits from the wealth of its land, no matter who is acting as its steward. This may become particularly relevant in countries where foreign corporations and governments have acquired large areas, as freehold or on long lease, to ensure their national security in food and biofuels.

Another advantage of stewardship fees and taxes on land is that they may be collected at any geographical scale. There is no need for a global tax authority or international agreements, welcome as these may be, and although they are normally described as collected at national level they can equally well be collected at the level of the parish or local authority.

Certain and convenient

Adam Smith's second maxim of taxation requires that:

'The tax which each individual is bound to pay ought to be certain, and not arbitrary. The time of payment, the manner of payment, the quantity to be paid, ought all to be clear and plain to the contributor, and to every other person' (1776: Volume III Book V Chapter II:208).

Smith's main concern was that lack of clarity can lead to insolence and corruption on the part of the tax-gatherer.

Tax collection has moved on since Adam Smith's day and modern taxes are certain in principle, although their complexity means that it is only people with special expertise who can feel completely certain. Yearly changes and temporary tax breaks mean that the certainty that does exist does not extend far into the future, and people and companies may find themselves subject to unexpected tax burdens. In the UK, examples include the withdrawal of tax relief on mortgage interest payments; changes to the tax regime for pension funds; and the rumours of a Stamp Duty holiday that temporarily paralysed the housing market in 2008.

A particularly serious transgression of the principle of certainty is the retrospective introduction of 'windfall taxes' on the profits of the oil industry or privatised utilities. This is 'arbitrary and uncertain' and erodes trust in government. It's not easy in practice to distinguish 'excessive' profit from 'normal' profit, and uncertainty about future taxation regimes distorts investment decisions.

Related to the issue of certainty is the issue of transparency. No one knows how much tax their friends and neighbours pay, nor the firms they work for and buy from. This lack of transparency adds to the sense of uncertainty and unfairness. Most people are aware of rafts of specially negotiated exemptions, exceptions and loopholes that are applied to a range of taxes, and of the extent of tax avoidance, particularly by the wealthy. This undermines confidence in a tax system that may appear incomprehensible, arbitrary and unfair.

In a stewardship economy the valuation of sites on which there are improvements depends on the professional valuation of these improvements and the result cannot be completely predictable or certain to the steward or even to other professional valuers.

The stewardship fees are determined by the market when a property is transferred from one steward to another. And they are updated regularly by professional valuers. There is recourse to appeal at any time to the market which provides a mechanism, though not a result, that is certain. Stewardship also makes the amount of tax visible, and certain, to 'every other person' through a publicly available database.

Smith's third maxim requires that:

'Every tax ought to be levied at the time, or in the manner in which it is most likely to be convenient for the contributor to pay it' (1776: Volume III Book V Chapter II:209).

Taxes should be levied at the same time as any income becomes available to pay them. If a tax levied in advance of income this deprives the taxpayer of cash-flow and puts barriers in the way of payment; if in arrears the temptation is to overspend and then panic when the tax is due.

The inconvenience, rather than the financial burden, of paying taxes is a less serious issue in ownership economies than it was in Adam Smith's day; PAYE and National Insurance contributions are particularly convenient for employees as they are deducted directly from their salary, and tax is deducted from many sorts of interest at source.

But most people's experience of participating in tax gathering is that it is far more intrusive and annoying than might be expected from the time taken. This is particularly the case where businesses are asked to collect taxes, such as VAT and sales taxes on behalf of the state. This money is the property of the state, so businesses must justify and explain both their accounting and their diligence in collecting the tax. Inspections are frequently carried out in a way that is challenging and confrontational. Sometimes inspection goes beyond the business - in Italy, tax policemen may check that retail customers have kept their receipts, as they are required to do by law (Economist 3/5/97). It can be unpleasant for tax-gatherers too – in Russia in 1996, 26 were killed in the course of their work, four were kidnapped and 41 had their homes burnt down (Economist 31/5/97:19).

If a property is rented out in a stewardship economy, it will generate an income stream to pay the stewardship fees which will be due monthly. But for steward-occupiers, who receive no rent, paying stewardship fees is as inconvenient as mortgage payments or rent in an ownership economy. This could be minimised by ensuring that the Universal Income is paid out each month just a few days before the stewardship fees are scheduled to be paid, or by deducting stewardship fees from a person's salary if they prefer.

The stewards who will find their stewardship fees most inconvenient, and most burdensome, are those whose land is not being used. In general, this should encourage people to bring underused land into use. But it could act as a disincentive to developers who need to assemble many plots of land to go ahead with a viable development and have to invest a good deal before seeing any returns. This requires special consideration.

The US Tax code is a document of nearly 10,000 pages, and the US Inland Revenue Service issues 582 different tax forms (Economist 15/4/06). The UK has more than 8000 pages of primary tax legislation, second only to India amongst the largest economies. One of the reasons for the complexity of the current tax system, and the consequent sense of unfairness, is that the government uses tax breaks, allowances and rebates to support good causes and policy objectives. This is much less visible to the general population than providing similar levels of support as subsidies or other forms of government spending. It encourages constant lobbying by special interest groups and provides opportunities for patronage and political favours. Tax breaks are not applicable in a stewardship economy where stewardship fees have replaced conventional taxes as a source of government revenue.

Efficient use of marginal land

If we imagine an ownership economy without taxes, land in the figure below ranges from highly productive on the left to unproductive on the right. The land that is shaded dark is beyond the margin of production: it is not put to use because the return is not enough to pay the wages and interest.

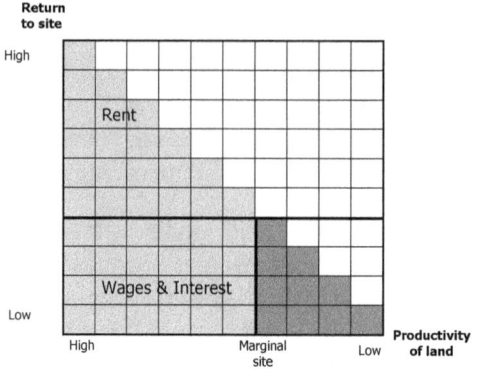

Fig 6. (based on Tommas Graves 2011)

The figure below shows the situation in which taxes have been introduced, at 50 per cent of wages and interest. Some sites that were previously used for production no longer have a high enough return to pay the total cost of tax, wages and interest and they fall out of use:

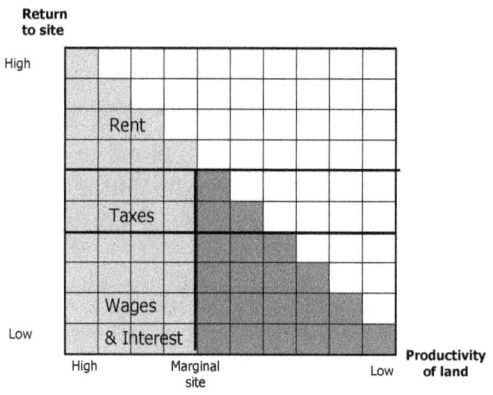

Fig 7. (based on Tommas Graves 2011)

The figure below shows the situation in a stewardship economy, where stewardship fees have been introduced that are equal to 50 per cent of the rent. As it falls less heavily on less productive than on more productive land, and not at all on marginal land, it allows production to continue at all the sites on which it occurred when there were no taxes.

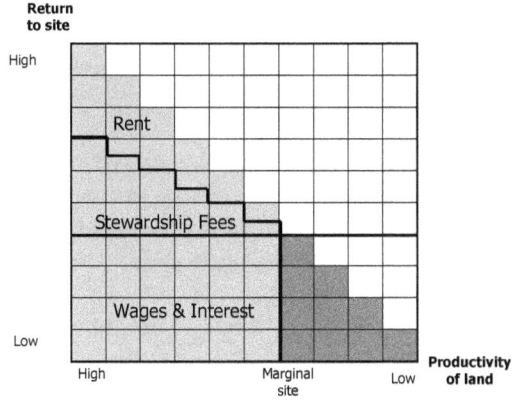

Fig 8. (based on Tommas Graves 2011)

Whereas conventional taxes increase the amount of land that is unable to support production as it is beyond the margin, stewardship fees have no such effect. More land is in use in a stewardship economy, supporting more people in employment.

Efficient land market

In an efficient land market taxation would encourage people to make use of or to sell underused land; there would be no tax on land transactions; transparent and accessible information would be available about past land sales and there would be no unnecessary delays in reaching a sale.

Taxation

The tax system provides little or no incentive to sell under-used land in an ownership economy. The failure to tax ground rents causes the market rent of land to rise, the market value of land to rise and speculative holding of land which generates a financial return.

In an ownership economy the element of the National Non-Domestic (Business) Rates that falls on the land is somewhat less than half the market rent of that land; this provides a reasonable incentive to make efficient use of the land or to sell it if it is not being used well, although not as much incentive as a tax of 100% on the market rent of land would do. The National Non-Domestic

(Business) Rates, however, contain numerous exemptions and reliefs, most importantly for under-used, derelict and agricultural land which are subject to no economic incentive to sell if they are not being well used (Julian Pratt 2014: 10).

Council Tax provides even less incentive to sell underused domestic land as it taxes an even lower proportion of the market rent of the land (particularly for high-value properties) and is also subject to numerous exemptions and reliefs – hence, for example, the million empty homes.

In addition, the Stamp Duty Land Tax discourages buying and selling of land, particularly when a seller believes that they might one day want to use the land even when they are not putting it to use at present.

In a stewardship economy no one holds land for speculative purposes and there is a strong financial incentive (stewardship fees equal to 100 per cent of the market rent of all land) to sell any land that is not being optimally used.

Even during transition to a full stewardship economy, stewardship fees would capture a higher proportion of the market rent than in an ownership economy and so provide a greater incentive to dispose of under-used land.

A stewardship economy is free from transaction taxes on land, so the land market itself exhibits less friction.

Information

In the past information about the availability of property on the market was held almost exclusively by individual estate agents and valuers. They too held information about the price for which properties had been sold in the past, along with the Land Registry. Little of this information was available to the general public. This situation has improved considerably over the last couple of decades, but it is still difficult and costly to access even a partial database.

The New Land Market in a stewardship economy requires that information about all properties currently on the market be freely available to all. The Land Registry would contain information about the price of the improvements on each plot, the most recent date on which stewardship fees were established in the open market and the current stewardship fees. For taxation is to be open and transparent, it will be necessary for this database be freely available to all.

Waiting for a sale

Land, and particular houses, can remain on the market for many years. This may be due to poor marketing but is most likely to be due to the seller asking too high a price for the property. Even when a price can be rapidly agreed, there are often long delays before contracts are exchanged.

In a stewardship economy the seller of a property is keenly interested in the valuation of the improvements on their plot, as this is the sum they will be paid. They have no financial interest in the stewardship fees offered by purchasers. This means that, once a seller has decided to sell, the time needed to reach a sale is only that needed to allow a reasonable number of potential buyers to come forward, plus the time that they need to satisfy themselves about the physical and legal condition of the property. The discipline of the auction in the New Land Market means that potential purchasers will take steps to satisfy themselves about these issues before rather than after their bid has been accepted.

❑ When stewardship fees replace existing taxes they bring about more efficient use of land, particularly where this is close to the margin of profitability.

❑ Conventional forms of taxation are not economically efficient – they impose a deadweight loss on the economy and distort economic decision-making. They are not efficient to collect as collection is costly and taxes are often avoided or evaded

❑ Stewardship fees as a single form of taxation are cheaper to collect, more difficult to evade and avoid, more transparent and introduce, and there is no deadweight loss or economic distortions.

❑ Stewardship fees are neither as certain nor as convenient as conventional taxes, but these disadvantages are relatively minor compared with the advantages in efficiency and fairness.

Chapter 4　　　Stewardship fees are fairer than taxation

How would you judge whether a tax, or a charge like stewardship fees, is fair?

In an ownership economy, where people believe that ownership of the natural world is no different from ownership of artefacts, no one form of taxation is any fairer than another. Here the least unfair way of arranging taxation is to have many different taxes, each bearing on different groups of people, so that no one escapes.

In an established stewardship economy, the stewardship fees do not take from an individual anything that is rightly theirs. The fees are a charge for the right to use the land and the environment and so may be seen to be fair.

Transition from an ownership to a stewardship economy does pose challenges and has to be very carefully designed if it is to avoid transgressing existing property rights and be fair.

'Tax' carries several meanings including a 'payment compulsorily collected from individuals or firms by central or local government' (Oxford Dictionary of Economics) and also 'an oppressive or burdensome charge, obligation or duty' (Shorter Oxford English Dictionary).

Libertarians believe that the role of the state should be minimal and that there is no justification for taxes, which represent the confiscation of private property (Murray Rothbart 1974). Stewardship fees are a charge not a tax, but it is natural to compare them with conventional taxes as they provide an alternative source of government revenue.

Criteria for fair taxation

Adam Smith's first maxim states that:

'The subjects of every state ought to contribute towards the support of the government, as nearly as possible, in proportion to their respective abilities; that is, in proportion to the revenue which they respectively enjoy under the protection of the state. The expense of government to the individuals of a great nation, is like the expense of management to the joint tenants of a great estate, who are all obliged to contribute in proportion to their respective interests in the estate' (1776: Volume III Book V Chapter II:208).

This maxim has been interpreted to refer to two different aspects of fairness, the 'ability to pay' principle and the 'benefit' principle. Three further aspects of fairness are considered in this chapter – the principles of sustainability, non-confiscation and gender equality.

The 'ability to pay' principle

Adam Smith makes explicit his view that taxation should fall equally on the three factors of production: land, labour and capital. One interpretation of the 'ability to pay' principle would be a tax that is proportional to all income, whether this be from land, labour or capital.

Another interpretation of 'ability to pay' is a tax that takes away from the taxpayer only what can be 'spared'. A poor person has little or nothing to spare once they have purchased the necessities of life, while a rich person has much more. The amount of income that can be 'spared' after paying for necessities rises with income more than in proportion to the income. Economists generally accept that to meet the 'ability to pay' principle a tax should be progressive - that is, the rich should contribute not just a greater amount but a greater proportion of their income than the poor.

Adam Smith was not averse to the idea of progressive taxation. He discussed a tax on 'house rent' (the rent for unimproved land plus rental from improvements) in the following terms:

'A tax upon house-rents, therefore, would in general fall heaviest upon the rich; and in this sort of inequality there would not, perhaps, be anything very unreasonable. It is not very unreasonable that the rich should contribute to the publick expense, not only in proportion to their revenue, but something more than in that proportion' (1776 Volume III Book V Chapter II:236).

The 'benefit' principle

The other aspect of Adam Smith's first maxim is the 'benefit' principle. Taxes should bear upon individuals 'in proportion to the revenue which they respectively enjoy under the protection of the state'. There are many ways of thinking of the benefit principle. If you interpret the 'benefit' simply as the person's income in the economy that is protected by the state, the benefit principle is no different from the 'ability to pay' principle. But if 'benefit' is understood to include all the goods and services provided by the state, the benefit principle might suggest that those who benefit from government action should pay for them. This might include tolls for the roads, local poll tax for street lighting and cleaning, direct charges for medical care and education, a national poll tax for defence and so on. If everyone benefits equally from street cleaning, for example, the rich will pay a smaller proportion of their income. Even if adjustment is made for the greater benefit that the rich gain from government action (e.g., police, defence or health care), this interpretation of the 'benefit' principle could lead to regressive taxation where the rich contribute a lower *proportion* of their income than the poor.

Sustainability

One way of judging whether our way of life is sustainable is whether our actions leave future generations at a disadvantage compared with our own. In the light of increasing environmental concerns and the possible role of taxation in mitigating these, an additional 21st century criterion for taxation is the extent to which it promotes sustainability. In ownership economies, environmental taxes may promote sustainable development, but most taxes do not have this effect.

Economic freedom

It is rare to find someone who is opposed to liberty, but the nature of this liberty, or freedom, divides us. Classical (19th century) liberals and libertarians stress that liberty is rooted in economic freedom, in particular private property rights and freedom from government intervention. They advocate low levels of taxation on the grounds that taxes restrict market freedom by confiscating things that people should be free to keep for themselves – income, profits, sales, value added and so on.

The principle of economic freedom as applied to taxation is that the state should not confiscate from individuals anything that is rightfully theirs. If a tax is levied on some thing or activity that is not 'owned' by any individual but by society as a whole, this may be seen as the fairest form of taxation. The principle of economic freedom, or non-confiscation, is not helpful when comparing taxes in ownership economies because all conventional taxes fail to meet the principle. Stewardship opens up the space for economic freedom to be a useful, indeed the primary, principle because it asserts that the market rent of the natural world cannot be owned by its steward. In an established stewardship economy, it is not confiscation to take what belongs to everyone and use it for their benefit, particularly in the form of a Universal Income.

Gender equality

Feminist economists have rightly proposed that governments, when enacting budgetary changes, should provide an impact statement detailing the consequences for men and for women – gender budgeting. Most of the cuts in spending imposed by the government's austerity programme from 2010 – 2020 are projected to fall on women, and gender budgeting exposes this. Impacts of tax cuts contribute to this through the consequent reduction in spending (Economist 25/2/17:70). Although there are aspects of the tax system that particularly impact women, for example the way that income tax is applied to single people and to couples, these are less significant than overall levels of taxation and spending.

Are conventional taxes fair?

Many conventional taxes are accepted not because they are perceived to be fair but because, particularly in combination, they are perceived to be less unfair than the alternatives. The following table summarises the extent to which different taxes, and stewardship fees, meet the various criteria for fairness.

Tax on	Example	Ability to pay	Benefit	Sustain-ability	Economic freedom (non-confiscation)
Wages	Income Tax National Insurance	Yes	Possibly	No	No
Interest	Income Tax Capital Gains Tax	Yes	Possibly	No	No
Poll	Community Charge	No	Possibly	No	No
Wealth	Capital transfer taxes Inheritance Tax	Yes	Possibly	No	No
Goods & Services	VAT Sales Excise Duties	No	No	Possibly	No
Capital gains	Capital Gains Tax	Yes	No	No	No
Production	Corporation Tax	Yes	Yes	No	No
Flat Tax (with annual exemptions)		Yes	No	No	No
Foreign exchange	Tobin	Yes	No	No	No
Environment	Carbon, landfill				
Market rent of land	Stewardship fees	Limited sense	Yes	Yes	Yes

The 'ability to pay' principle

The 'flat tax', which taxes all income at an equal rate, is an attempt to meet the interpretation of strict proportionality. Most examples of a flat tax on income include a personal allowance that is exempt from tax. This is intended to remove the poorest from taxation and ensures that it is closer to the ability to pay.

Taxes on goods and services like VAT do not meet the 'ability to pay' principle because they take a higher proportion of the income of the poor. Taxes on wealth are usually considered to meet the 'ability to pay' principle. This may not be reasonable, especially when the item being transferred by gift or inheritance cannot be divided and must be sold to provide the wherewithal to pay the tax. A poll tax fails completely to meet this principle.

Taxes on wages, rent, interest and production are usually implemented in a way that is progressive and are therefore usually considered to meet the 'ability to pay' principle.

The fairness of a tax depends as much on the exemptions from taxation as on the rate of taxation. In some jurisdictions the imputed or notional rent paid by an owner-occupier to themselves is subject to Income Tax, though that has not been the case in the UK since the removal of Schedule A Income Tax in 1963. Capital gains on owner-occupied properties are, however, exempt from Capital Gains Tax in the UK. Indeed, exemptions from Capital Gains Tax destroy the progressive nature of Income Tax. Taxes on income cannot be considered in isolation from taxes on capital gains, not just out of a sense of fairness but because firms can choose whether to reward their shareholders with income or capital gains, and their staff with income or stock options, and will exploit any discrepancy between the tax rates.

In the UK in 2009 Capital Gains Tax started at 18 per cent while the top rate of Income Tax was increased to 50 per cent.

The 'benefit' principle

A flat-rate Income Tax at the national level, combined with a Poll Tax to pay for services provided by (local) government, could meet the benefit principle if these were the only taxes.

Sustainability

Taxes on wages and interest do not promote sustainable development. Taxes on goods and services can be used to promote sustainable development when they are targeted at activities that harm the environment.

Non-confiscation

This principle is particularly important to liberals and libertarians, who emphasise individual autonomy and rights. If someone owns something, any tax levied on it, or the income derived from it, can be considered to be a form of confiscation. Libertarians also regard taxes on labour as a form of confiscation. John Locke stressed the importance of self-ownership, according to which each individual owns their own body in the same way that they own artefacts. Self-ownership underlies the New Right and libertarian thinking of Ayn Rand and Robert Nozick. It has proved to be a useful way of resisting the will of others, whether that of individuals or of the state. In the economic realm it suggests that people have the right to the whole of the product of their own labour.

The principle of non-confiscation is of less concern to socialists, who accept the potential for taxes to go some way towards achieving transfers 'from each according to his ability, to each according to his need' (Louis Blanc 1848).

All forms of taxation with which we are familiar are then, to some extent, a form of confiscation.

In all economies those born rich tend to stay rich and those born poor tend to pass on their disadvantage down the generations. This has led to all manner of attempts to break this cycle. Taxes on transfers of wealth between the generations were levied by the Egyptians in the 7th century BCE and have been a matter of controversy ever since.

It has proved difficult to design a fair way to implement an Inheritance Tax. In the UK about 5 per cent of the population pay Inheritance Tax, and this group own about 40 per cent of the national wealth. The current threshold in the UK of £325,000 (2010) does ensure that it is only the wealthy who pay and so it seems much fairer than VAT on domestic fuel, to take just one example of a tax that falls disproportionately on the poor. But the very rich avoid Inheritance Tax through sophisticated tax planning using legal loopholes and offshore companies. It is middle-class home-owners who bear the brunt of Inheritance Tax, particularly when they die unexpectedly. A former chancellor of the exchequer, Roy Jenkins, described it as a 'voluntary levy paid by those who distrust their heirs more than they dislike the Inland Revenue'. Perhaps it would be more generous to describe it as a tax on the unlucky and those who fail to get good tax advice.

Inheritance Taxes are not applied everywhere and have been abolished in Sweden, Italy, Canada and Australia. It's not surprising that there is a range of strong opinions about Inheritance Tax, particularly amongst home-owners. Libertarians describe it as a 'death tax' that robs people at the moment of death and causes the break-up of family farms and businesses; and indeed, in the USA and UK it does fall on the estate.

Supporters of Inheritance Tax, including socialists and some liberals, consider it as a tax on unearned income that is paid by the heirs to an estate. This is the form it takes in most other high-consumption economies. The heirs inherit the resources to pay it and the revenue offers the possibility, through government spending on the relief of child poverty, of giving everyone a slightly fairer start in life.

Gender equality

Since women tend to have lower incomes than men, regressive taxes such as Council Tax, National Insurance contributions and VAT tend to be particularly damaging for women.

Since none of the taxes so far described meets the non-confiscation principle, conventional taxation needs packages of taxes that are the least. This means making sure that taxes draw on each of the arms of the circular flow and thus fall on everyone as equally as possible, no matter what the nature or source of their wealth.

Probably the best-known advice about taxation, reportedly given to Louis XIV by his treasurer Jean-Baptiste Colbert (1619-1683), advocated a combination of taxes on very pragmatic grounds:

'The art of taxation consists in so plucking the goose as to obtain the largest amount of feathers with the least possible amount of hissing'.

In the UK about 80 per cent of taxes currently fall on work and enterprise, 12 per cent on natural resources and 8 per cent on others (including alcohol and tobacco). What is the result?

'If I have worked harder and built myself a good house while you have been contented to live in a hovel, the tax-gatherer now comes annually to make me pay a penalty for my energy and industry, by taxing me more than you. If I have saved while you wasted, I am mulct [subject to taxation], while you are exempt. If a man build a ship we make him pay for his temerity, as though he had done an injury to the state; if a railroad be opened, down comes the tax-collector on it, as though it were a public nuisance; if a manufactory be erected we levy upon it an annual sum which would go far towards making a handsome profit. We say we want capital, but if anyone accumulate it, or bring it among us, we charge him for it as though we were giving him a privilege. We punish with a tax the man who covers barren fields with ripening grain; we fine him who puts up machinery, and him who drains a swamp' (Henry George 1879 Book IX Chapter I:390).

In an ideal world the state would raise the revenue that it needs in a way that does not take from anyone anything that they rightly own – taxes would be non-confiscatory. If that criterion can't be met, other considerations come in to play. An ideal system of taxation would ensure that each person's payments supported a sustainable economy and gender equality; that payments were more or less in line with the benefits that each person gets from being part of a complex economy, and that they are in a position to pay the amounts required.

Are Stewardship fees fair?

The 'benefit' principle

Revenues from land have supported the state throughout most of history, from Sumeria through ancient Greece to 18th century Europe. In England, Income Tax was not introduced until 1799 when landowners successfully resisted shouldering the burden of paying for the Napoleonic Wars. Support for taxes on land as a major, or indeed sole, source of revenue has never gone away, and most countries levy at least a small amount of tax on land values.

Places of worship, learning and healing have, in many cultures, been financed by the rents of the land that they own. This is the funding mechanism advocated by Islam. The value of landholdings of the colleges of Oxford and Cambridge amounted to £3.5 billion in 2018 (The Guardian, 29 May 2018) with income supporting teaching and research.

Land values in an ownership economy, and stewardship fees in a stewardship economy, reflect the value of the services provided to that land by society, enterprise and the state such as transport, security, employment, education and so on.

Adam Smith stated: 'The subjects of every state ought to contribute towards the support of the government, as nearly as possible, in proportion to their respective abilities; that is, in proportion to the revenue [services] which they respectively enjoy under the protection of the state....' (Book V Chapter 2.) In a stewardship economy this is precisely mirrored by the market rent of the land to which the state grants them exclusive use. It is difficult to imagine a closer fit of any tax to the 'benefit' principle.

The 'ability to pay' principle

Commercial, industrial and agricultural land has a market rent because it can be put to profitable use. Here stewardship fees meet the 'ability to pay' principle precisely. The same applies to residential property that is let to a tenant. But for residential property that is not let, stewardship fees may fail to meet the 'ability to pay' principle. The steward in this case may not have an income stream to pay the tax. If we assume that the government in a stewardship economy raises the same taxes and has the same level of expenditure as it currently does, then stewards who have higher than average per capita land value will not be reimbursed as much in Universal Income as they pay in stewardship fees.

The rich can, if they choose, largely avoid the tax by living in a relatively undesirable place and not using significant amounts of land or environmental resources in their business activities (Stewardship Economy: FAQ A millionaire). Few rich people would choose to live in that way, but if they did it is not self-evident why we should tax them simply because they can afford it, given that sufficient revenue is available from a non-confiscatory source.

By and large, stewards of high-value properties will have a source of income, or at least a stock of wealth, to enable them to pay their stewardship fees. But there is a problem for people who have got used to living on a low income in an expensive location, particularly during transition to a stewardship economy, which needs to be carefully designed (book 1: FAQ A widow living in a large house).

Sustainability

Environmental damage to a steward's plot of land results in a downward assessment of the improvement value, and there is a financial incentive in a stewardship economy to care for the land. Stewardship makes a major contribution to sustainability by levying environmental charges for activities that damage the environment. However, stewardship may apply pressure to overdevelop the land, and this needs to be counteracted by the planning system.

Non-confiscation

From the perspective of an ownership economy, taxation of land is just as much confiscation as is taxation of goods. Taxation of 100 per cent of the annual market rent of land looks like outright confiscation of land.

Stewardship is based on a different understanding – that the natural world cannot be owned. According to this view the annual stewardship fees in an established stewardship economy only collect from the steward what anyway belongs to everyone. If the principle of stewardship rather than ownership is accepted, stewardship fees have the overwhelming ethical advantage that it is the only form of taxation to fully meet the 'non-confiscation' principle.

Gender equality

Men own more land, and more valuable land, than women and so stewardship fees would be likely to benefit women.

A form of poll tax?

The underlying principle of stewardship is that the revenue from stewardship fees is to be used for the common good, as government revenue or to provide a Universal Income. One way to achieve this is for the government to state in its manifesto how much revenue it needs for its proposed policies and for the rest to be distributed as a Universal Income. But another option is to allocate the whole sum as a Universal Income and then to collect an equal Poll Tax from everyone. The former is probably the clearest route, but interestingly they are formally equivalent.

A single tax?

The primary purpose of stewardship is not the redistribution of wealth or the reduction of inequalities, although it would contribute significantly to both. Its purpose is to make a fair share of the wealth of the natural world available to everyone. At the same time, it fully respects the ownership of what belongs to individuals.

In a stewardship economy there would be no need to impose other taxes - including those on income (earned and unearned), firms, VAT etc. Indeed, when orthodox taxes are introduced into a fully developed stewardship economy they would raise no additional revenue – the tax taken would reduce people's ability to pay rent for their land and so reduce stewardship fees. Taxes would be imposed with the sole intention of changing behaviour.

Liberals and socialists would probably impose 'sin taxes' to change personal behaviour that is judged to be undesirable – like smoking and drinking. Socialists might add Inheritance Taxes to reduce inequalities that persist across the generations in ownership societies. Libertarian versions of stewardship would probably impose no other taxes at all.

The idea of a 'single tax' on land and natural resources has always met resistance. One reason, no doubt, is the memory that the Physiocrats in 18th century France believed that the only source of wealth was agriculture, and that agricultural land should provide the only basis for taxation – 'l'impôt unique'. This emphasis on agricultural land became less and less relevant as the industrial revolution progressed.

The other reason for resistance to a single tax is the idea's association with the very influential Single Tax movement in 19th century America. Henry George advocated a Land Value Tax amounting to a large enough percentage of the market rent to allow the replacement of all other taxes and appeared to suggest that it be introduced immediately (1879 Book VIII Chapter II:364). The effect of this would be to transfer the whole burden of taxation onto one class of society – landowners. Although *Stewardship Economy* and its associated books describe a steady-state stewardship economy that is based exactly on Henry George's proposal, it does not advocate a rapid transition.

Stewardship Economy describes what a stewardship economy might be like in an ideal world. In such a world a 'single tax' disadvantages no group - certainly not 'landowners' as there are none.

Part II The Role of the State

Chapter 5 The role of the state

Stewardship is most likely to be adopted at the scale of a state, as it is the state that is responsible for preserving territorial integrity and the wellbeing of its citizens as well as authorising and enforcing property rights. The Land Stewardship Trust collects stewardship fees for the benefit of the whole population. It does so primarily to allocate land in a fair way. The state uses part of the revenue to fund government expenditure and makes the rest available for distribution as a Universal Income. There is a range of possible roles that the state could take on. Political choices would be as important, and as controversial, as in ownership economies.

How can we ensure that the state does not take on unnecessary functions that erode the value of the Universal Income? What is the balance between the power, and expenditure, of local and national government? And, to take one example that may be informed by stewardship, how should the state allocate monopoly rights when these are in its gift?

The years leading up to 2008 were a time when the private sector (particularly the banks, the wider financial services industry and also the car industry) profited hugely from the expansion of credit. When they were at risk of failure they were judged 'too big to fail' and were bailed out by the taxpayer. Profits had been privatised but the losses were then socialised, and to pay for this it is public services not the banks that have undergone cuts.

In more recent years we have seen the failure of many large private sector companies in the field of construction, railway provision, security, prisons and residential care. These failures have included bankruptcies, renegotiation of franchises or simply withdrawal from the market and have frequently been preceded by directors and shareholders paying themselves excessive rewards, firms failing to contribute to their pension schemes and leaving subcontractors unpaid. They have always left the public sector to provide the essential services that the state cannot walk away from in the same way that a private sector company can.

After these experiences it is impossible for most people to give any credence to arguments that free unregulated markets know best. The question is no longer how to reduce the size of the state, but what are its appropriate functions.

Ownership economy

Limits to the size of the state

The role and size of the state is a keenly contested political issue. In an ownership economy the level of government spending is limited by the tolerance of the electorate for taxation.

At local government level it is much less straightforward to trace a direct link between the electorate and levels of local authority spending. One reason is that most of the revenue used to fund local spending is collected not by local government but by central government and passed on to local government in the form of the Revenue Support Grant (which replaced the Rate Support Grant). Another reason is that significant numbers of electors are not making a direct financial contribution to local government funds as they receive Council Tax Benefit. Both of these factors make local authorities less responsive to the concerns of local electors about the level of local taxation than would be the case if local electors paid for a greater proportion of local expenditure.

Functions of the state

Guardian and contractual functions

Jane Jacobs (1992) provides a language for thinking about the appropriate role of the state that builds on Plato's distinction in the *Republic* (Plato. and Lee, 1974) between *commercial* occupations, which supply people's needs; and *guardian* occupations, which protect the state from corruption within and from enemies without.

Her 'commercial' (contractual) syndrome is described as the moral code appropriate to trade, commerce and production, as well as to science. It is the moral code appropriate to organisations that are seeking mutually beneficial voluntary agreements. This includes the market, at least in its ideal form.

54

The 'guardian' syndrome is the moral code appropriate to work that protects one's 'own' territory and people from 'others'. This applies within the state as well as in disputes between states – Cicero held that the state is founded mainly to protect private property (De Officiis I 21-22). The archetypal guardian is a warrior or politician who is prepared to use force or trickery to defend the territory. More generally, this is the moral syndrome appropriate to any group that exerts prowess – that has power and uses it effectively. This morality is appropriate to those who maintain the territory internally (police, emergency services, judiciary); those who govern it (government, civil service); and those who safeguard the health and well-being of people (environmental health, public health) and of the environment (planning, resource monitoring).

The guardian syndrome provides a framework within which commercial activity can flourish. This requires the state to suppress violence, mandate honesty, enforce contracts, promote competitive markets, regulate business – and establish enforceable property rights.

One possible implication of the dichotomy between guardian and contractual moralities is the proposal that the state should take on only guardian functions and avoid functions that require contractual morality.

Managing externalities

Many aspects of the environment have been poorly managed in ownership economies. The cost of damage to the environment from pollution or extraction has not been borne by the polluter but by the environment and therefore by all of us: the cost has been externalised. The state is responsible for protecting its territory from this sort of damage. It may choose to fulfil this responsibility by enacting regulatory measures. It may encourage those who use the environment to self-organise to manage the environment as common property. It may manage the environment directly. Problems have most frequently arisen when the environment has been treated as an open access regime.

One approach that has probably not been used enough is to create private property rights in the use of the environment – for example the emissions permits that have been developed for CO_2. Where the state chooses the private property rights approach, decisions about the number of permits to issue are guardian, not contractual, functions. Once the property rights have been established the market will put a price on them that ensures that polluters internalise the costs. The state then needs to take on the guardian role of enforcing the surrender of permits by polluters.

The opposite problem arises if benefits, rather than costs, are externalised. For example, homeowners close to a park or businesses close to a railway hub benefit from the increase in the value of their property from these amenities, but no one has a financial incentive to provide the efficient amount of parks or railways. The state needs to ensure that these providers (of parks, transport and so on) are able to internalise the benefits themselves, such as the increase in land value, and reap some of the reward.

Rescuing private enterprise from failure

The failure of a firm is hard for workers and investors, but it is an essential aspect of the market economy, as the possibility of failure selects our less successful business plans. When failure occurs, it allows resources to be re-allocated to more profitable enterprises and permits the waves of creative destruction that Joseph Schumpeter identified as driving innovation.

Some enterprises, however, are too big and too important to be allowed to fail. Examples are those that are critical for the life and health of individuals and for the smooth running of our complex society – the banking system, the internet, utilities, the system of food production and distribution, the transport system and healthcare. The state needs to secure their survival, and not necessarily through long-term nationalisation. The lesson from the banking failures should surely be that the state need feel no responsibility to intervene before the enterprise goes into receivership, and no responsibility for the shareholders, but should provide a guarantee that it will buy the enterprise from the receivers and keep it running as a going concern. The difficulty is how to know where this blends into the behaviour of a corporate state that inappropriately tries to shape the functioning of the economy through subsidies and/or protectionist measures to support domestic enterprise.

Provider monopolies

Where there is just one provider in a market (a monopoly provider), it can control the supply of a particular product or service and so can determine its price. Where there are few providers (an oligopoly) they too can control the price, for example by forming a cartel. The problem with monopolies from the point of view of the consumer is that they are able to maximise their profit by selling a smaller amount of their product at a higher price than if there were competition. From the point of view of the business, monopolies may become bureaucratic and inefficient and cease to innovate in the absence of competition.

The usual response from the state is to break up monopolies or prevent them from forming by using competition law. But does it always make sense to duplicate fibre-optic cable networks, or mobile phone reception masts, or production facilities? We should be able to find ways of making the most of monopolies when this is appropriate.

Monopolies can have real advantages, as shown by the 'ice-cream vendor's problem/dilemma'. One ice-cream vendor will place herself in the middle of a beach to reduce the distance that customers need to walk. A second, competitive ice-cream vendor will place herself close to the first, at the middle of the beach. A monopolist controlling both ice-cream vendors would spread them along the beach, thereby minimising the distance that customers walk and so maximising customer satisfaction and sales. The disadvantages of competition were vividly illustrated by the deregulation of buses in the 1980s, when each bus tried to arrive just before its competitor.

A monopoly may be granted intentionally by the state, imposed by a single firm which uses its size to crush other firms, or it may arise directly or indirectly from land ownership.

Bookmakers' pitches provide an example of land forming the basis for a monopoly, or oligopoly. This illustrates the role of land in many monopolies. The most attractive pitches for bookmakers at the races are those that are closest to the stands. Pitches used to be allocated by the National Association of Bookmakers using the 'dead man's shoes' rule; when a bookmaker retires the pitch was offered to his son, daughter or wife. If they did not take it up the other bookmakers moved closer to the stands and the least desirable pitch was made available. Under this system the pitches were not allocated efficiently to those who really wanted them and were able to make best use of them, sometimes outsiders had to wait 25 years to get a pitch (Economist 2/11/96:36).

These positions on the bookmakers' seniority list were allowed to become tradable property rights. Pitches in some cases have changed hands for over £1 million and represented the major assets of many small bookmaking firms. Just as with fishing quotas and land ownership, these property rights were understood to be held in perpetuity. This system of property rights gifts the market rent of each pitch to its incumbent, depriving the racecourse of income that would be available if the pitches were auctioned each year. This system was threatened in 2007 when the Racecourse Association announced that from 2012 it would no longer recognise bookmakers' list positions, but individual racecourses have subsequently reached agreements with their bookmakers that retain the seniority list in return for increased payments by bookmakers.

Since monopolies can maximise their profits by producing smaller quantities at a higher price than if operating in a competitive market, market economies need to take steps to regulate and control them. This is likely to involve the property system. Many monopolies or oligopolies have their origins in land ownership. Land ownership itself is often described as a monopoly right – not necessarily forming the basis for a producer monopoly, but often offering that possibility unless many identical plots are available. Even where land ownership does not provide a business monopoly at national level, key assets such as a port, airports or mine will often provide the basis for a local monopoly.

Brian Hodgkinson (2008:55) points out that ownership of a single site can establish monopolies well beyond the boundaries of that site. Such a monopoly may be local, as in the case of a shop in the middle of a housing estate with poor or expensive public transport connections to the main shopping area. It may be regional, for example where the owner of a port grants access to the port and preferential trading arrangements in a way that sets up monopolies in its industrial hinterland. And it may be national, where the location of the source of raw material may form the basis of monopoly supply through vertical integration.

Land lies at the centre of lesser degrees of imperfect competition. The theory of perfect competition assumes that the costs faced by all producers are ultimately the same once each has developed the most efficient way to produce any particular item. This theory explicitly ignores the persistent differences in production costs that characterise production on real sites – for example sites at differing distance from their raw materials, labour, energy sources and market. Economic theory generally tends to ignore geography.

A 'natural monopoly' arises where a single firm can produce all the output for which there is demand at a lower cost than a combination of firms. The most obvious examples are utilities like the supply of gas, electricity, water and (until the advent of mobile phones) telephones. It is usually said that the basis of these monopolies is the large, fixed investment (the networks of pipes and cables) that a competitor would not be able to justify duplicating. But the basis of these monopolies are networks of land, and it is the ownership of this land as much as the capital invested in equipment that underlies the monopoly.

The state can grant a wide range of monopoly rights such as business monopolies, the right to create money and intellectual property rights. It may do so to increase the returns to a risky or strategically important venture or to reward a favoured individual or corporation. But it may be because a monopoly is the best way to provide a service efficiently – a natural monopoly. The state may choose to operate the monopoly itself or to delegate this task to the private sector.

Public sector

The most direct form of public ownership is one in which the service is directly managed by the state – for example the armed forces. State ownership and management was widely adopted after World War II but came to be seen as inefficient, lacking in innovation, unresponsive to the recipients of services and dominated by the interests of public sector trade unions. One approach to making the direct management of public services more 'business-like' has been to reward the management team according to some measure of their performance by means of a performance contract, for example, the banks that were taken into public ownership around 2008.

From the beginning of the Thatcher government in 1979 until the financial crash of 2007 directly managed public services were widely regarded as second-best to the private sector, although the rationale for privatisation was recognised to be ideological rather than evidence-based and a minority continued to advocate public ownership. As public support for renationalisation grows (see below) it is important to recognise the burdens imposed on state-owned activities that at times seem to outweigh the cost to private sector providers of the stream of dividends and excessive rewards for directors. These include the limitation of revenue as services expand, the disincentive to investment as it increases public sector debt, the requirement to continue to provide services, the responsibility to a wide group of stakeholders, the additional requirements imposed by the public sector and the attention given to public services by the media.

When a private sector company provides goods or services that are popular it acquires a stream of revenue that allows it to provide these goods and services. If it can convince itself that a new line of goods and services will generate new revenue, it can justify the investment needed to provide them. A public sector provider, on the other hand, finds itself increasingly stretched when its goods or services prove popular, as it often needs to try to continue to provide them without any new resources. This is particularly problematic when increased demand is driven by demographic change (e.g., the demands on the NHS by an ageing population), or technological advance (e.g., improved forms of health care) or economic development (e.g. infrastructure provision).

Public sector provision needs a source of funding that grows as demand for its goods or services grows. The government needs to balance its books so that its expenditure is equal to its income. But it also needs to be able to invest in projects that generate long-term benefits, such as infrastructure.

Public sector spending needs to be separated into current spending and investment for the future. Examples current spending include the situation its current income is less than its current expenditure or where it is repaying interest on debt. Investment for the future may be needed for infrastructure and training. A different accounting mechanism may be employed, but the ideal approach is to ensure that investment results in increased revenue to the government.

Public sector monopolies are, almost by definition, essential services that cannot simply be withdrawn. We can cope without baked beans but not without a railway system or a health service. So public sector providers must operate in such a way that they can continue in business indefinitely. This means living within the budget allocated by government and cutting their provision accordingly. This conflicts with the statutory responsibilities to provide services, which in combination with responsibilities to other stakeholders impose huge management burdens on public sector managers.

Where services are privatised or contracted out, the private sector contract has no comparable responsibilities. The government is generally unwilling to force private sector companies into liquidation and so they renegotiate contracts in favour of the private sector providers. And if the worst comes to the worst, the private sector provider is protected by the limited liability of its shareholders.

As public services need to be provided by organisations that will continue unbroken provision, companies with limited liability may not be suitable for public sector provision.

If a private sector company is contracted to provide school meals, for example, and it can do so profitably and within its contract by providing poor nutrition, it is perfectly reasonable for it to do so. If a provider owned and managed by the state takes this approach it is failing in its fundamental purpose – to serve the public good. Providing nutritious food is an integral aspect of providing a positive educational experience, not least because children learn better when they are not hungry.

Each public service should be aware of serving the whole of the public good and its many stakeholders including customers, workers, suppliers, the community and the environment. This increases the complexity of management in the public sector and the cost of provision. These responsibilities to stakeholders need to be the same for any provider of public services whether they are public or private sector.

The public sector is rightly subject to reporting requirements that are designed to reduce the risk of corruption and to increase transparency and accountability. Particularly onerous are the contracting requirements, designed with the good intention of preventing cronyism. In the private sector an efficient company will source its consumables from whoever offers the lowest price for a product that appears to meet the specification. But where it is seeking a provider for a complex set of services it will identify reliable suppliers and subcontractors largely on the basis of their past performance and reliability and continue to use them. In such a situation both purchaser and provider will regard their relationship as a long-term investment and tend to treat each other well rather than beat each other down point by point and contract by contract.

It is difficult to know how to minimise the risks and costs of these requirements, but where the private sector is drawn in to public sector provision it must meet the same requirements for things like disclosure of conflicts of interest, openness to freedom of information requests and so on.

Whether run by private sector or public sector providers, public services will inevitably attract far more media attention than the provision of private goods and services.

Private sector

When the state transfers monopoly provider rights to the private sector it may do so as a permanent transfer of ownership or as a time-limited franchise. A franchise will need to be managed against the contract that forms the basis of the franchise, private sector ownership will need to be subject to regulation so that the provision serves the public good.

Since 1979 there has been a drive to privatise public services as the result of a belief that the private sector and the discipline of competition would necessarily produce more customer-focused and efficient operations. In this model the monopoly right is transferred into private ownership and closely regulated against specified quality standards, levels of investment, price and so on by means of a regulatory contract.

In this model the monopoly right is retained in public ownership but licensed to a private company for a defined period of time by means of franchising – for example the spectrum auctions, national lottery or the train operating companies. To put in place a franchise, a regulatory body for the industry sets standards that will apply for the duration of the franchise – maximum prices, quality standards and so on. Providers who want to apply for the franchise go through a prequalification process to identify those who are judged capable of running it successfully. A time-limited franchise is then awarded to the highest bidder.

Franchising can provide the consumer with the benefits of a planned service. It also ensures that the monopolist is required to behave competitively and captures the monopoly profits for the benefit of society. However, many operating franchises have performed poorly, particularly the train operating companies who have been allowed to renegotiate their contract rather than carry the cost when it became clear that the provider had won the franchise by making overoptimistic assumptions of passenger growth; examples were Virgin and Stagecoach on the East Coast Mainline in 2018.

Construction is a notoriously risky business and there have inevitably been contracts that led to the collapse of a supplier, for example, the construction of hospitals in Liverpool and Birmingham undertaken by Carillion at the time of its failure in 2018.   One of the problems of company collapse is that the company is able to go into receivership and shed its responsibility for fulfilling its contract. Sometimes this borders on the farcical, as when Serco announced that it was not, after all, able to provide security for the London 2012 Olympics. But where this involves the provision of residential and nursing home care, as in the case of Four Seasons, failure leaves vulnerable individuals at risk of being thrown out of what is their own home.

The UK Private Finance Initiative has proved to be the most extreme example of the unfortunate hybrid of private and public sector. Introduced in 1992, it was an attempt to improve the country's infrastructure by taking investment off the government's books (disguising its own borrowing) without transgressing the European Union's (1992) Maastricht treaty provisions that limit a country's Public Sector Borrowing Requirement (PSBR). Each PFI initiative bundled a large construction project such as a school, hospital or prison with a long-term (e.g., 30 years) contract to operate the facility. The contracts appear to have been written in such a way that, while the profits are privatised, the risks are socialised (National Audit Office, 2018).

Private provision of public sector projects and services, whether short-term or long-term, risks imposing major costs on society; these include inadequate pay for workers, excessive pay for directors, the raiding of pension funds and the collapse of providers with or without their taxpayer bailouts.

Although it is claimed that it is the greater efficiency of private providers that enables them to bid to provide services at lower cost than public providers, the reality is that most of their advantage comes from paying their workers less, both in basic pay and in benefits like sick pay and holidays. This approach to pay inevitably leads to resentment by workers who are unable to provide as good and as flexible a service as they would be if they were paid more.

But even more damaging, is the impact of low pay on the economy as a whole. Pay in many industries is so low that it does not, on its own, provide enough to sustain workers and their families, who have to claim in-work top-up payments in the form of Tax Credits. Apart from the inefficiency of so many people having to claim and administer these benefits, this cost should be added to the more obvious costs incurred to the government. The damage is not limited to current income; low paid workers need additional subsidies, for example, for housing, and are less able to support themselves in retirement.

Workers are not the only stakeholders who have repeatedly been treated shabbily by corporations. Sub-contractors' invoices are often routinely paid three or four months after they are received, causing, at best, cashflow problems and at worst insolvency if late payment pushes the organisation into administration. The environment may be exploited, and the public deprived of good, reliable services.

Even if it were possible to believe that privately owned providers could be much more efficient than publicly owned ones, it has always stretched the imagination that this would be enough to provide generous dividends for shareholders and high levels of bonuses for directors. This distribution of the assets of corporations has directly contributed to the public disquiet with private sector corporations providing services to the state. The impact has been amplified by events like the collapse of Carillion in 2018 with an estimated £800 million pension deficit.

Unfortunately, the high level of reward for directors and shareholders has been provided in part by the failure of many corporations to meet their obligations to contribute to the pension funds of their workers. This may be at no greater a level than in the private sector as a whole but it adds to the costs to society.

Both the collapse of a provider and its prevention by state bail-out impose a cost on the state.

Corporate structure

There have been many proposals for the reform of company law, including a requirement for workers on the boards of all corporations, an increase in the number of co-operative and not-for-profit entities and a clear statement of the purpose of a corporation above and beyond delivering (short-term) shareholder value.

But there are even more fundamental reforms required, of which the most important is to remove the limited liability status of large companies that take on government franchises and contracts. Such a reform would be a step too far for small and new firms, which need to be able to grow without threat to the livelihoods of their founders and shareholders, but a company that is responsible for large government contracts and potentially 'too big to fail' needs also to take responsibility for carrying out its contracts and bailing itself out. With responsibility falling on the shareholders, it is more likely that contract bidding and business plans would be more realistic. This single reform would produce a much more level playing field between public and private sector providers.

Stewardship economy

Any society, including a stewardship economy, that puts individuals in guardian roles must develop systems of accountability. These may include the democratic process and a free press; systems for detecting and punishing corruption; and a positive ethic of public service based on respect and adequate remuneration.

A stewardship economy needs to place limits on government expenditure. There are certain minimum levels of state activity that would be required to maintain a stewardship economy, and options for the provision of public goods. In managing the private sector, it would need to manage externalities, rescue private enterprise from collapse and manage monopolies.

Minimum requirements for the state

Institutions are sets of rules, procedures and norms that prescribe, proscribe or permit particular actions. Political institutions may impact on economic relationships in many ways, for example by defining the nature of property rights and the rules of exchange (James Caporaso and David Levine 1992:149).

A stewardship economy needs at least the following institutional functions:

Administering stewardship of land

- ❏ Maintaining a register of property rights to land and the environment.
- ❏ Valuing and monitoring improvements, particularly buildings, and environmental damage.
- ❏ Administering a new land market in which properties are transferred at auction.
- ❏ Collecting stewardship fees.
- ❏ Evicting stewards who do not pay the stewardship fees.

Administering stewardship of the environment

- ❏ Deciding how many environmental permits to issue.
- ❏ Administering permit auctions.
- ❏ Enforcing the surrender of permits when the environment is used.

Universal Income and Environmental Dividend

- ❏ Distribution of Universal Income and Environmental Dividend.

Planning

- ❏ Land use planning.

Legislature

❑ Legislature to make and change laws, including those relating to stewardship.

Legal system

❑ A legal system capable, at the very least, of resolving disputes about stewardship including enforcement of payment of the stewardship fees and of planning restrictions as well as the protection of stewardship rights. More generally there have to be mechanisms to enforce property rights and contracts.

Police

❑ A police function capable, at the very least, of enforcing the decisions of the legal system.

Defence

❑ A means of defending its territorial integrity (and protecting the rights of its stewards).

Other functions of the state

It would be possible to implement stewardship in a state that has these minimum functions, or in one that also takes on additional roles.

The most significant impact of political institutions is the way they shape the role of the state. In ownership economies political parties differ strongly in the role they advocate for the state, and in a stewardship economy the opportunities for difference are just as great. Governments of different political hues would adopt different versions of stewardship.

Liberal and socialist versions of stewardship might want the state to take on most guardian activities. They might also want the state to take on a limited range of contractual functions, while socialist versions would be more likely to favour state ownership. Libertarian versions would limit themselves to the minimum requirements set out above.

The usual reasons given for the state to intervene in commercial and contractual arenas, in addition to its role in planning and regulation, are to correct information failure; to correct market failure; to provide public goods; to manage externalities; to protect private enterprise from collapse; and to manage monopolies.

Stewardship provides a remedy for one significant information failure that is widespread in ownership economies – the lack of readily available information about the current market rent of all land.

'Market failure' describes inefficiencies that arise in markets from a variety of causes including externalities, under-provision of public goods and monopolies. Where market failure takes the form of under-provision, the root cause is generally the inequalities in wealth that mean that poor people cannot exert 'demand' in the market: much as they may need something, they may not have the resources to bid for it. This under-provision may be remedied by ensuring that wealth is more evenly distributed in society, although it does not rule out other approaches to correction such as state ownership.

Public goods   – things like street lighting and defence but also education, health and social care, law and order and the arts may not be provided by market mechanisms . Socialists and liberals would favour state provision of these goods while libertarians may believe that they should be left to private, voluntary or charitable provision.

If the state does take responsibility for providing public goods in a stewardship economy, it feels fairer than it does in an ownership economy. This is because revenue is raised from stewardship fees, which belong to all of us, not from taxes on enterprise and work. For example, street lighting increases the market rent (stewardship fees) of local properties and if there were no means of national defence, land values would fall. Charges on the value of land are the natural way to pay for the provision of public goods.

Markets only have a chance of allocating resources efficiently if there are private property rights in those resources and if there are no costs or benefits that are off the balance sheet of those involved in the market transactions, that is, externalised.

Stewardship ensures that most of the natural world - the environment as well as land - is not managed as an open access regime. Both the state and private proprietors are required to act as stewards and pay stewardship fees to the Land Stewardship Trust for any land they hold, causing them to question the wisdom of retaining its landholdings.

Costs are internalised, because the polluter has to pay the true cost of the damage – true cost pricing. Benefits, too, are internalised. Where public benefit is revealed by the rising stewardship fees from land, for example when there is new transport provision, the public benefit can be captured and internalised as a subsidy to the transport provider (Stewardship Economy: Why?: Chapter 14). And where it is not possible to internalise these costs and benefits, the state in a stewardship economy has the option of directly providing a range of public services.

The state in a stewardship economy needs to make only very limited use of subsidies and bail-outs, but it would be within the principles of stewardship for it to take over selected assets of businesses that are in receivership.

Putting limits on government expenditure

Stewardship fees equal to the market rent of land have the potential to raise large amounts of revenue. The risk in a stewardship economy is that this would allow state expenditure to grow, reducing the level of the Universal Income and leading to some unwise decisions about public works, as illustrated in the Land Tax enclave of Fairhope in the U.S, founded in 1894 (Huntington 1922). Municipal investment there was initially directed, perhaps very appropriately, to the construction of a landing stage that facilitated coastal trade. It later extended to running a ferry service, a risky venture that might more appropriately have been carried out by the private sector – as became apparent when the ferry was wrecked. Later still, as the revenue from the land taxes rolled in, the town installed an early telephone system for which there was little demand, and which was eaten by rats.

The challenge is to provide adequate revenue for both national and local government while ensuring that neither level spends in a profligate way. One approach that meets this challenge is for the Land Stewardship Trust to collect stewardship fees in each area, pool them in a national pot and distribute the funds both between local and national levels and between revenue for the state and a Universal Income. This would be accompanied by the removal of the Revenue Support Grant, so all local spending was financed from local stewardship fees.

Each local authority would decide how much revenue it needs to provide locally appropriate services and seeks election on the basis of a binding request for its budget. The Land Stewardship Trust compares authorities by their per capita spending request and allocates the maximum per capita amount requested by any local authority across the whole country. Local authorities with lower spending needs than the maximum would have a surplus, which they would distribute as a local Universal Income.

This would ensure that areas in need of higher spending receive it, but that their electors would understand that this results in their receiving a lower local Universal Income than if their local council spent less. Local political parties would offer different packages of services and local Universal Income, allowing electors to decide what level of spending they want but understanding the personal cost.

The remainder of the national pot of stewardship fees would be available to the national government with each political party standing for office having to make a binding budget request in its manifesto. If elected, this is the amount that the Land Stewardship Trust would pay to the government. As with local government, the state receives the revenue that it needs for its programme and the remainder is distributed as a national Universal Income. The electorate makes an informed choice between state spending and the national Universal Income.

This proposal could transform electoral politics, as it would mean that each party would have to present a budget for its proposed activities. If it fell into deficit, a government could call an election requesting an increase for its budget or borrow money on the open market, for which it would be held to account at the next election. Surpluses and deficits would be carried over from one administration to the next, and the incoming government would have to include in its budget a sum to repay any outstanding debt.

There are many questions to be answered; for example, the budget available to a coalition that forms after an election which might perhaps be the weighted sum (by votes received) of the spending plans of the members of the coalition. But it is possible to imagine that governments could be held to account for their levels of spending. The key is to keep government spending quite separate from the process of collecting stewardship fees and distributing the Universal Income.

Monopolies

The stewardship approach offers a way of thinking about property rights to a site that can be usefully applied to other monopoly rights. A firm may exercise a monopoly right provided that the monopoly rent is captured for the benefit of all.

In a stewardship economy the state's function in relation to any monopoly that it creates is to ensure that it is used effectively and for the maximum benefit of society; that it captures the monopoly rent for the benefit of everyone, rather than allow this to be appropriated into private hands; and that it protects the rights of the monopolist to any improvements that they make.

Economists use the term 'rent' (or 'economic rent') with a wider meaning than it has in *Stewardship Economy: private property without private ownership*, to refer to the difference between the amount that a factor of production (land, labour or capital) is actually paid and the amount it would need to be paid to remain in its current use. One example of economic rent is the additional profit generated when a producer has a monopoly. This is greater than the normal profit it would earn in a competitive market and is called 'monopoly profit'. Franchising captures for public benefit the economic rent arising from a monopoly and auctioning franchises to operate state-granted monopolies is a natural approach in a stewardship economy if the state does not choose to manage the monopoly under direct state ownership.

The parallels with the capture of the market rent of land in a stewardship economy are clear. The standards imposed by the regulator are the equivalent of planning restrictions on land – and if the regulator imposes low user prices or high-quality standards, the value of the franchise is lower, and society receives less revenue. Just as with the stewardship of land, it is important to ensure at the end of the franchise that the operator does not lose the value of any improvements it has made.

A site like a port may have a high market rent as the result of the local monopoly that it enjoys. This market rent is collected as stewardship fees and returned to the community. The role of the state is to require the Land Stewardship Trust to revalue the site at annual intervals, which may necessitate periodically exposing it to the market (in the same way that train operating franchises are currently allocated). This ensures that the operator of the monopoly is exposed to competition – not from other operators actually running a competing business but - from potential operators who could imagine operating the monopoly more or less profitably and thus would bid higher or lower stewardship fees. In this way, where a monopoly is the most efficient form of enterprise, it remains a monopoly but distributes its monopoly rent to everyone.

The Land Stewardship Trust allocates monopoly rights to plots of land, including networks of land used by transport systems, and collects stewardship fees. The Environment Stewardship Trust allocates monopoly rights to the environment, including utility networks, and collects charges or fees.

Chapter 6　　　Investing in transport infrastructure

Infrastructure, for example transport infrastructure, improves business efficiency, labour productivity and Gross Domestic Product (GDP). Investment in public transport also reduces inequalities in income, and reduces the environmental damage caused by transport.

When a government funds transport infrastructure from general taxation this may feel unfair. Why should we all, as taxpayers, pay for local transport measures in parts of the country that we may never visit? It might seem fair if everyone benefited equally, but transport systems always have different impacts at different locations. Why can't the people who benefit meet the cost of the infrastructure?

This chapter suggests that infrastructure can become locally self-funding by laying claim to revenue from the increase in the market rent of the land that benefits from its provision.

Ownership economy

In ownership economies the costs of constructing and operating transport infrastructure fall on both users and the taxpayer. In addition, ways have been found to extract contributions from the other group who benefit from good transport connections – those who benefit from an increase in the value of their land.

Operating costs

The operating costs of transport systems include labour, maintenance, ticketing and the rental or capital costs of both fixed and mobile infrastructure. All or part of these costs may be met from charges to the direct users through ticket prices and tolls, though the transport operator is often able to provide the level of service that society wants only as the result of a state subsidy – that is to say, transport provision is prone to suffer from market failure.

Construction costs

Even when the revenue from fares is enough to meet the operating costs of transport provision, it is generally not enough to service the debt incurred in making an investment in transport infrastructure. The return on capital that investors anticipate is often not realised. Early investors in the canals, railways and the channel tunnel all saw the value of their shares fall dramatically (Fred Harrison 2006a). This has meant that governments have often had to step in to fund transport infrastructure because it provides a public good.

When the fullest possible assessment of the costs and benefits is carried out, the benefits may significantly outweigh the costs. The canals and railways were failures only for their investors. The landlords, who were the original sponsors of the schemes, were the real beneficiaries. Their mines and businesses flourished, and the market rent of their land soared, as their cost of transport to market fell. Many of them sold their transport shares on to a wider group of investors and it was these shareholders who lost out as the gains in land values were external to the finances of the canal and railway companies (Fred Harrison 2006a).

Infrastructure increases land values

The people who most obviously benefit from transport infrastructure are those who use it, and this is reflected in their willingness to pay to travel. But there are other beneficiaries including firms, workers, customers and landowners.

The value of a plot of land depends above all on its location and reflects the sum of all the services and opportunities that are available at that location. The improved job opportunities, trading opportunities, and quality of life provided by the transport infrastructure all increase the desirability of living and producing in this location.

When land becomes more desirable because of improved transport connections, its value rises. Building plots are worth more when they are served by roads. And when a rail link is built between a suburb and its city centre people living in the suburb can more easily work in the city centre, the suburb becomes a more desirable place to live and the land values rise. The city centre becomes more accessible to workers, clients, customers and suppliers and land values rise there too. Landowners are the main financial beneficiaries in an ownership economy.

Not all landowners, however, gain from transport infrastructure. Negative impacts are also translated into land values – properties along a railway line may have higher levels of noise and pollution and this may reduce their value even if properties near stations rise in value. But for a well-conceived scheme the overall benefits outweigh the costs.

The idea of funding the development of transport infrastructure from the anticipated increase in land values has a long history. A witness to the Standing Committee on Metropolitan Communication suggested in 1845 that 40-year loans for transport infrastructure should be secured on the rise in rateable value of nearby property (Nicholas Crafts and Timothy Leunig 2006: 33).

In his illuminating book on self-funding transport infrastructure *Wheels of Fortune*, Fred Harrison describes the 1988 plans for the development of Canary Wharf in London's Docklands (Fred Harrison 2006a:64). The developers, Olympia and York, estimated that a new underground line to bring commuting workers from Waterloo and London Bridge main line stations would increase the market rent of the office space by £320 million per year, equivalent to an increase in its capital value of £3.2 billion. The estimates they obtained for the construction of the underground line were less than £600 million, and at this price they were willing to foot most of the bill for construction and hand the infrastructure over to the public sector to run. This solution foundered for several reasons including the increasing ambition of the scheme, disagreements about shares of funding, delays and ultimately an economic recession that dramatically reduced the demand for office space and so also reduced its projected market rent.

The proposed underground line was eventually completed in 1999 as the Jubilee line extension. Don Riley, a property developer with interests in the area, estimated in his book *Taken for a ride* (Don Riley 2001:23) that it raised property prices around the stations by £13 billion, more than three times its eventual construction cost.

Fred Harrison (1983) provides numerous examples of the increased land values resulting from infrastructure developments in ownership economies, including the Hokuso railway in Tokyo, the Metro in Washington and the Docklands Light Railway in London.

He also describes how speculative rises in land values can choke off development before it takes place. But measuring the change in land values associated with infrastructure developments is not easy and may in some cases demonstrate little or no change in land values. This was the case for the Sheffield and Croydon tram systems (RICS 2004), where local residents may not have viewed them as well-conceived infrastructure.

In ownership economies it is transport users and landowners who benefit from infrastructure investment, whether this is funded from private or public sources. If the transport provider relies for its income from transport users alone the venture may well not meet its costs and will either fail or require government subsidy. This suggests that we should capture the increase in land value that arises from the provision of well-conceived transport infrastructure, and use this revenue to subsidise transport investment and, if necessary, running costs.

Development of transport may lead to an appreciable acceleration in economic growth and that under-investment in transport in the United Kingdom may have weakened economic growth (Nicholas Crafts & Timothy Leunig 2005:51). The Confederation of British Industry (CBI) believes that transport is one of the top three issues that will determine the UK's future competitiveness (CBI, 2017). In his report to the Treasury, Rod Eddington (2006) identified seven mechanisms by which transport improvements improve business efficiency, the economy and GDP:

- Business is more efficient because of time savings and improved reliability. This means that fewer resources are required to do the same job – you need half as many buses to maintain the same frequency if the journey time is halved, for example.

- Workers have better access to jobs – people can travel further to find suitable jobs, so labour is more flexible and labour markets more efficient.

- Competition is enhanced as products and services are delivered in a more timely way to a wider area.

- Domestic and international trade increases.

- Business and investment is attracted to the UK.

- Economies of scale and new ways of working are made possible, particularly for supply chains and logistics with approaches like 'just in time' manufacturing and 'warehousing on wheels'.

- Productivity improves through improved business-to-business connections, which support clusters and agglomerations of economic activity.

Rod Eddington identified that the annual costs to UK business of unreliability on the rail network was £0.4bn and road congestion around £7-8bn. His study modelled several possible future scenarios, in all of which the costs of congestion are projected to rise significantly. The central scenario suggested that congestion would increase by about 30 per cent by 2025, causing increased costs to business of over £10 billion a year and costs to households through wasted time of another £12 billion a year. This modelling suggests that a reduction in congestion that cuts travel times by 5 per cent for business and freight travel on the roads could generate about £2.5 billion in immediate annual cost savings, equivalent to 0.2 per cent of GDP (Rod Eddington 2006:1).

The benefits of investing in public transport go much wider than these benefits to business and GDP, including reductions in:

- inequalities, by enabling poorer people to travel
- casualties and property loss from road traffic accidents
- greenhouse gas emissions.

One approach to travel congestion is to build more roads or airport terminals. Eddington provided an overview of transport investment projects that have been subjected to cost-benefit studies. He argued that in the UK there is little justification for investment in completely new transport links, although his dismissal of high-speed rail links and enthusiasm for short-haul flights may reflect the perspective of the airline industry and does not incorporate the full greenhouse implications of aviation fuel.

Eddington identified a range of situations where gains may be had from encouraging behaviour change, making better use of existing assets or investing in variable capacity like increased bus frequencies or longer trains. Increased congestion is already indicating where new investment in modest schemes would make a difference, and many of these have benefit-cost ratios exceeding

10:1. These include small-scale walking and cycling schemes; and schemes to tackle road bottlenecks, particularly in urban areas and their catchments, inter-urban corridors and around ports and airports.

In an ownership economy there is a particular problem associated with funding for infrastructure because the taxes required themselves impose a deadweight loss on the economy. To be worthwhile, investments that are funded by taxation have to bring benefits that are much greater than the costs.

Eddington made several important recommendations about the need both to reform the planning process for transport infrastructure and to ensure that sub-national transport decision-making bodies have the powers and scope to handle decisions across all modes of transport. However, the experience of increasing capacity is that, if it does not impose a cost on the user, it simply stimulates people to travel longer distances more frequently until the new capacity is full and more is again needed. True cost pricing provides a way to manage demand for transport.

True cost pricing for transport

The true cost of a road journey includes the cost of the damage it does, including congestion and the emission of greenhouse gases. These costs are shifted onto others (externalised) in an ownership economy.

Eddington notes that congestion is limited to certain times and places and suggests that the most effective way to reduce congestion is to manage demand at peak travel times. His key point is the need to base all transport decisions on the balance of benefits and costs. The way to shape individual travel decisions and guide investment is to 'get the prices right'. The way to do this is for all travellers to pay the true cost of their travel, including the congestion they create and the environmental damage they cause.

Roads

How will we respond to the higher cost of motoring as oil prices rise? We might, of course, choose to travel less. But there is a range of alternative ways of making more efficient use of the roads including coaches, minibuses, shared taxis, car pools, lift-sharing and hitch-hiking.

A road in an ownership society is generally treated as an open access regime, but it can be actively managed either as common property or through private property rights. Commoners might ration access, as in Athens when cars with a licence plate ending in an even number were allowed to enter on even number dates and those with an odd number on odd number dates. Or, the right to drive at a time when the road is congested might be sold for a fee that could be fixed, related to the time of day or set dynamically to reflect the current degree of congestion. We are, after all, used to paying higher prices for goods and services at peak times - not just for rail and air tickets but for telephone calls, cinema tickets and so on.

Eddington's modelling suggests that a well-targeted road pricing scheme could reduce congestion by some 50 per cent below the central forecast for 2025. This could be expected to generate annual GDP benefits of £15 billion and total annual benefits of £28bn, although the implementation costs are unknown. These benefits require road travel to cost a maximum of 80p/kilometre at the busiest of times, including the costs of carbon (Rod Eddington 2006:39-40).

Even for journeys that coincide with the rail network, 85 per cent of journeys (passenger miles) in the UK are made by car. There is not enough spare capacity on the railways to accommodate this extra load. At normal occupancy a bus or coach uses only 20 per cent of the fuel per passenger compared with cars, and, at 60 miles per hour, carries as many passengers as a mile of cars. Coaches are safer, no slower and they release time for leisure and work particularly when they are supplied with legroom, mains power, Wi-Fi and video.

For intercity travel, Alan Stanley (2007:22) has advocated a coach network in which transfers take place at motorway intersections and connect with shuttle services to city centres. Land at the intersections would be used for services, offices, meeting rooms and hotels and its value, and stewardship fees, would rise.

Air travel

Airports were not congested until the middle of the 20th century. Runways that had at first been open access regimes were transformed into common property with the airlines as commoners, initially left to themselves to agree how to allocate take-off and landing 'slots'.

In the European Union these slots now attract a charge according to a set tariff which is set well below its commercial value. To deal with the resulting excess demand airport scheduling committees, originally formed by airlines to avoid clashes of timetables, allocate the slots according to a set of rules. The most important rule is 'grandfathering' – if you had the slot last year you get it again this year. (This parallels land ownership – whoever squats the land gets to keep it indefinitely.) There are additional rules to make sure that use is made of slots, including the 'use it or lose it' rule that leads to some underused slots being returned to the 'pool' each year. There is a great deal of exchange and barter. This exchange is necessary because the value of any slot depends on the whole bundle of slots the airline requires – not just a take-off slot but an earlier landing slot at the same airport and a later landing slot at the destination, as well as suitable access to embarkation gates, baggage handling, refuelling and catering.

The ultimate power to allocate the slots probably lies in the UK with the Civil Aviation Authority on behalf of the government, though the European Union also has some claim. These allocation mechanisms have disadvantages that are familiar and predictable. Slots at Heathrow are even more under-priced than at its rivals at Stansted and Gatwick, making Heathrow more attractive to both travellers (who pay less than the true cost price) and investors (whose businesses are subsidised), and increasing the pressure for development.

These property rights are valuable – the total value of slots at Heathrow was estimated to be worth $2.5 billion in 1997 (Economist 18/1/97:88). The property rights are not legally enforceable and there is no secondary market, or market prices, for the slots. This means that competing airlines which could make better use of the slots are unable to do so. And it prevents leasing or outright sale of slots (which would make it easier for new entrants to get a toehold if an airline's plans or its financial situation changes). Airlines currently have an excessive incentive to use their slots, even if the aircraft need to fly around empty, rather than lose them.

The European Commission has consulted on slot allocation and the British government favours market mechanisms and market prices. Their proposal is to establish a secondary market in which airlines buy and sell slots in a transparent manner and a primary auction process to allocate slots created by new capacity and those returned to the pool. These auctions would be for the right to use the slot for a defined number of years – the bids are to rent the slots not to own them outright.

When is it worth investing in transport infrastructure?

Benefit-cost ratios

The narrowest assessment of benefits and costs is the purely commercial one of revenue and expenditure. Will the revenue from fares and tolls exceed the operational and maintenance costs plus the cost of repaying the capital investment? But many of the important benefits, and indeed costs, are experienced by others beyond the transport operating companies. Internalising these benefits and costs requires, first of all, a method for attributing a price to them.

The benefit of infrastructure investment to travellers can be quantified by establishing what they are prepared to pay for their journeys, either by observing their response to charges or by asking them in choice experiments. But it is a challenging task to put monetary values on all the other benefits and to aggregate these into some measure of the total benefit.

The benefit-cost ratio (BCR) provides an estimate of the net value of the benefit generated for every £1 invested (Department for Transport 2012 accessed: 'New approach to appraisal'). In the UK this includes, in addition to revenue and expenditure, a monetary estimate of some additional social benefits such as the time saved, safety benefits and the costs of travel. It does not include GDP impacts or environmental costs or benefits.

The Department for Transport recommends that proposals for infrastructure investment should take, as the starting point for an assessment of their value for money, their benefit-cost ratio. The assessment is then adjusted to take into account non-monetised costs and benefits that include environmental and social impacts. Alternatively, a 'value for money benefit-cost ratio' incorporates monetary estimates of a wide range of social and environmental costs and benefits including GDP impacts, loss of amenity value of landscape and townscape, environmental damage to local air quality, greenhouse gas emissions, noise, accidents and congestion.

Value for money

In an ownership economy the deadweight loss of taxes on labour and enterprise depresses economic activity so any investment funded from general taxation must confer a substantial benefit to justify this loss.

In a private enterprise a real return on investment of 10 per cent, a ratio of benefits to costs of 1.1 to 1, would be worth considering. A government, mindful of its responsibility to manage the whole economy, can only invest if the benefits outweigh the costs to the economy as a whole, when the benefit-cost ratio is greater than 1.3 to 1 (assuming a deadweight loss of 30 per cent).

A project is judged to be:

- poor value for money if its BCR is less than 1 (loss-making)

- low value for money if its BCR is between 1 and 1.5 (a return on investment of up to 50 per cent)

- medium value for money if its BCR is between 1.5 and 2 (a return on investment of 50 - 100 per cent)

- high value for money if its BCR is over 2 (a return on investment of over 100 per cent (DfT 2012 accessed).

Stewardship economy

One way in which a stewardship economy influences transport provision is through the prices faced by travellers. The cost to travellers in a stewardship economy reflects the true cost of their journeys including their impact on congestion and greenhouse gas emissions.

Transport providers, like all sectors of the economy that release greenhouse gases in a stewardship economy, pay the true cost of the climate change that they cause. They pass this on to transport users, which reduces the demand for transport.

The impact of true cost pricing depends on the way in which the revenue from charges for congestion and carbon emissions is used, as described later in this chapter for road pricing. Broadly speaking, it would result in some combination of shifting travel to times of lower congestion; shifting modes of transport, for example from private car to public transport; and reducing distances travelled.

The abatement costs of cutting carbon emissions are higher for transport than for most other sources of CO_2 emissions (Stern, 2007) so transport is likely to be one of the last sectors of the economy to respond to true cost pricing of carbon by delivering cuts in emissions.

The element of the stewardship fees that is attributable to the transport infrastructure may be identified and reserved (hypothecated) for investment in the infrastructure, which later becomes self-funding. Where new infrastructure is planned, its benefits, of course, need to outweigh its costs in a stewardship economy, but the costs do not impose any deadweight loss as the revenue is raised from stewardship fees not taxes on income, profits and so on. The state in a stewardship economy would invest more in transport infrastructure because it could accept a 10 per cent return on investment rather than requiring a return of 50 per cent before a project is judged to be even of medium value for money.

An approach like this has been used in Copenhagen to finance its mass transit system (Tony Vickers 2007:30) from the Land Value Taxes anticipated from the development of the dockyards.

Rail

In a stewardship economy the idea of a stewardship trust is applied to the land, the environment and to infrastructure provision. There would be a stewardship trust for each mode of transport such as the roads, air, sea and, in this example, rail. The Rail Stewardship Trust holds in trust all the land that makes up the rail network.

In a libertarian version of stewardship, a transport stewardship trust like this might take the form of a franchise awarded at intervals by competitive tender. In a socialist version of stewardship, it might be a government body, and in a liberal version a not-for-profit arms-length body.

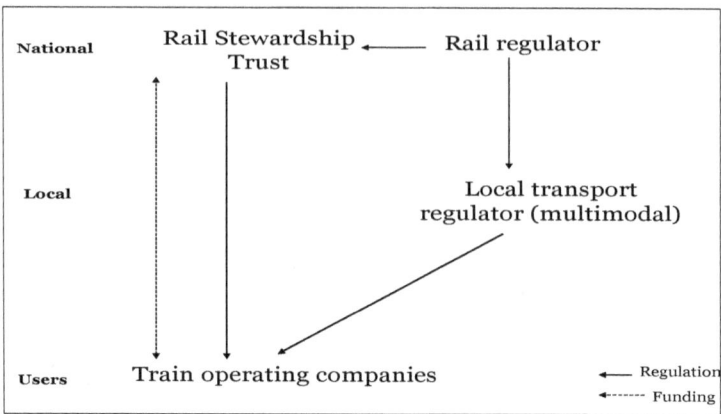

A transport stewardship trust is subject to the ruling of a specialist transport regulator for that mode of transport. The regulator stipulates fares, safety conditions and interoperability standards at a national level. At a local level the Rail Stewardship Trust is subject to a local multimodal regulator that ensures integration between all modes of transport and specifies service frequencies, connections and so on. This local regulatory function, like the local planning function for land, is located within local government.

Train operating companies and rolling stock leasing companies may be owned by the state, by private companies or by not-for-profit organisations and function in the same ways as in an ownership economy. A transport operating company does not have an indefinite right to run its services. At the outset and at regular intervals, say every five to ten years, the stewardship trust reallocates by auction the franchise to operate particular routes. Bidders go through a prequalification exercise to ensure that they are fit to run the service, and they guarantee to pay to the outgoing transport operating company the value of any improvements. The track, signalling and stations may be owned by train operating companies or by separate transport operating companies.

Each prospective transport operating company makes a bid which could be either an offer to pay, or a request for a subsidy, to run the franchise. If the best bid is for a subsidy, the stewardship trust needs to reassure itself that the transport operation does generate at least this amount of revenue from the additional stewardship fees of properties that benefit. If this is the case, the infrastructure is judged to be self-funding, and the bid for the lowest subsidy secures that subsidy along with the right and the responsibility to operate the network. If the transport operation is not judged to be self-funding the regulator does not offer the subsidy and the service closes.

Even where the revenue from fares is enough to meet the operating cost, it is often not enough to service the debt incurred when the transport infrastructure was put in place. Revenue from the additional stewardship fees attributable to the transport infrastructure, a measure of the wider social benefits of a development, can be used to fund investment as well as subsidising operations. The necessary steps are:

❑ The local transport regulator, the local office of the Transport Stewardship Trust and the transport operating companies discuss and agree candidate investment projects. In the case of rail this might be an entirely new line or upgrading that goes beyond routine maintenance such as electrification.

❑ The transport operating companies advance a business case for the project. This includes estimates of costs and of the anticipated rise in market rents of properties affected by the project.

❑ The local transport regulator scrutinises the business case.

❑ If the estimated increase in revenue from fares plus the increased stewardship fees is greater than the total cost of repayments and interest on the loan to fund the work plus the operating costs, the proposed investment is judged to be self-funding and may be approved as an investment that is expected to produce a financial return to the Land Stewardship Trust.

❑ The local regulator seeks agreement from the local office of the Land Stewardship Trust that it will provide a subsidy to the Rail Stewardship Trust of no more than the anticipated rise in stewardship fees. The Rail Stewardship Trust is then in a position to fund the investment.

Roads

In a stewardship economy road transport is more expensive but less congested. Congestion wastes fuel as well as time, so congestion charges reduce CO_2 emissions as well as congestion. Fuel prices reflect the cost of carbon permits, and there may be toll charges and parking charges.

The roads regulator sets the regulatory requirements (equivalent to planning conditions). These may include maximum charges and desired levels of unoccupied parking spaces.

In a stewardship economy the Roads Stewardship Trust is responsible for keeping congestion below some threshold set by the roads regulator. To do this it assesses the carrying capacity of the roads and, at times of day when it expects this capacity to be exceeded, levies charges that are high enough to keep the number of vehicles below the carrying capacity. These charges might be by hour, by day, or by mile and may be determined in advance or according to the current level of congestion. The roads regulator monitors congestion and imposes penalties on the Roads Stewardship Trust if congestion thresholds are exceeded or if charges are made unnecessarily.

The rationale for toll charges - charges to use a section of road – is to provide finance for building and repairing roads. Libertarians might accept that, since the Roads Stewardship Trust is the steward of the roads, it should be free to charge users whatever tolls it likes. Liberals might also allow the Roads Stewardship Trust to set their own tolls, but subject to caps agreed with the regulator. Socialists might make the roads available free of charge, or at low cost, to all.

In a stewardship economy the steward of each site charges whatever fees they deem appropriate for off-street parking. The Roads Stewardship Trust manages on-street parking. It might charge fees with the aim of maintaining a certain proportion of empty spaces – to reduce congestion of parking places. The levels of these fees may be subject to the ruling of the roads regulator.

The Roads Stewardship Trust may take a variety of forms, such as a limited company operating under franchise or a government department. It is responsible for building, maintaining and operating the roads and associated facilities such as service areas and bus and coach stations. It derives its revenue from congestion charges, tolls, parking charges and rent from service areas. It does not make any additional charges to motorists like road fund tax and does not receive any income from carbon permits. Its expenditure may include tracking systems, charging systems, traffic police and parking wardens as well as the physical structure of the roads.

The Roads Stewardship Trust's total income from charges may not be enough to meet its expenditure. In this case it will need to make a business case for a subsidy from the Land Stewardship Trust to be funded from stewardship fees. If the Roads Stewardship Trust makes a surplus, there are several options for the use of the funds. Any net income from toll charges is reserved for construction and maintenance of roads. Income from congestion and parking charges might be used in one or more of the following ways.

- One approach, which might be favoured by libertarians, is to ensure that charges paid by drivers are used to benefit drivers – for example redistributed in proportion to the number of miles driven each year. The impact of this would be to redistribute income from drivers who travel when congestion is low to drivers who travel at peak times. This applies pressure on *when* people travel, not on *how* they travel. On the other hand, the revenue could be used to fund investment in roads, which would reduce the need for toll charges.

- Another approach, which might be the choice of socialists, is to use the revenue from road users to invest in public transport, so ensuring that everyone has access to affordable transport. This redistributes income from drivers to those who might use public transport, particularly to those without cars. People are likely to respond by changing their mode of transport, but not by reducing the distances travelled.

- The revenue from congestion charges and parking could be distributed to the whole population as an Environmental Dividend, enabling them to meet at least part of the cost of whatever form of transport they choose. This would redistribute income to people who travel less and apply financial pressure to travel less. This might be favoured by liberals as it increases freedom of choice without requiring state intervention.

Buses and coaches

In a stewardship economy buses and coaches pay the same price for fuel as any other road user, thereby ensuring that there is a financial incentive to maximise fuel efficiency. They pay a congestion charge which would be only minimally higher than that for a car, reflecting the amount of road used by the vehicle travelling at its desired speed.

A bus or coach operating company may attract a subsidy in a stewardship economy, like a train operating company. As with railways, land values are increased at the places they connect.

Alan Stanley's motorway interchanges (2007) are the sort of self-funding transport facilities that could be funded from the stewardship fees of the businesses that move to cluster around them.

Air travel

In an established stewardship economy, an airport conducts a regular auction for the right to use each take-off and landing slot for a defined number of years. This allocates slots to the carriers who are prepared to pay the market rent, those who presumably value them most and can make best use of them. If a secondary market is allowed to develop, when an airline finds that it no longer needs a slot it can sell it or rent it for a time to another airline.

The airport needs to block anti-competitive practices that prevent open competition for slots in the auctions, just as in any auction with small numbers of bidders.

The auction of take-off and landing slots provides one of the income streams for the airport, along with revenues from parking, rental of space for retail outlets and so on. It is not easy to estimate the total stewardship fee that an airport should pay as there are no real comparables. One approach is to estimate the stewardship fees from knowledge of the airport's profitability using the receipts and expenditure, or profits, method of valuation. This approach is powerfully influenced by the auction price of landing slots. If this approach is not possible, it may be necessary to expose the airport to the market from time to time to establish the stewardship fees.

During a transition to stewardship the allocation of take-off and landing slots would require careful thought. Perhaps existing grandfathered rights could be converted into short leasehold rights with a duration of, say, seven years – a sort of 'sunset' arrangement. This would provide the airlines with a tradable asset while signalling the future requirement to pay the full market rent of the assets they are using.

In a stewardship economy the Air Travel Stewardship Trust allocates airspace to individual aircraft by means of its air traffic control system. Where the airspace is not congested the trust manages it as a common property regime. Where there is congestion, it auctions permits for use of that airspace in advance. If this does not raise enough revenue to meet its running costs it is funded by means of a levy on the stewardship fees of airports.

Waterways

Waterways are managed by Watershed Stewardship Trusts. They derive some of their income from permits – for moorings, for keeping a vessel on the waterway, for water supply – and some from renting space for infrastructure networks like fibreoptic cable under the towpath.

Utilities

Benefit-cost calculations and investment decisions, similar to those for transport infrastructure, must be made for the utilities. For many utilities, the so-called natural monopolies, it makes no sense to duplicate the provision of infrastructure for electricity, water, gas and sewage. The telephone network used to be a natural monopoly but is now subject to competition from mobile phone networks. Investment decisions for telecoms are most appropriately left to the private sector, within a regulatory framework.

In a stewardship economy each of the natural monopolies is held in Trust by a stewardship trust and is subject to a regulatory body in very much the same way as transport networks. The stewardship trust allocates franchises to the highest bidder. If the utility companies anticipate that they can operate at a profit they bid to make a payment. If they anticipate that they will run at a loss, they bid for a subsidy.

In the same way as with transport infrastructure, an operating or investment subsidy for utilities infrastructure projects is made available only if a business case can be made that this infrastructure will sufficiently increase the stewardship fees paid by the plots of land affected. This ensures that all infrastructure is self-funding.

Stewards who welcome improved infrastructure – and those who do not

In a stewardship economy appropriate investment in transport infrastructure leads to an increase in the value of land and so to an increase in stewardship fees. Most stewards of land that is affected by the infrastructure development will welcome its provision and accept the additional cost. Businesses will be able to pay this from the increased profits that the infrastructure brings, while householders will accept the cost for the additional utility that it provides. There will be some, however, who bear the costs but do not benefit.

A relatively small number of stewards will resist any proposed infrastructure investment because of the increased cost that this will impose. This is likely to be rare for businesses, as shown the voluntary supplementary business rate that contributed to the funding of Crossrail.

Householders are more likely to put up resistance. If they are themselves unlikely to make use of the infrastructure as they are being asked to pay higher stewardship fees for something they do not want. At its worst they may have to move home or see their area change as people who value the infrastructure, and can afford to pay for it, move in.

The position of householders close to the infrastructure is very different from what it would be in an ownership economy, where they would make a windfall gain as the value of their home increased. This is a real problem in for a stewardship economy but since a major purpose of a stewardship economy is to improve the efficiency with which land is used, the challenge can't be dodged. The most efficient use of land supplied with the new infrastructure is for it to be used by someone for whom the infrastructure is a significant asset. It is possible to put in place mitigating mechanisms during transition, such as rolling over payment of fees until the present occupant leaves the property. But as people adjusted to the multiple benefits of living in a stewardship economy their security would come less from owning a home that is rent-free and they would likely become more ready either to pay the increased fees or to move.

Self-funding transport

A business that is close to a transport link benefits from its ready access to markets, suppliers, other businesses and workers. The locational benefits enjoyed by its premises are reflected in the market rent of the land on which the business premises are located. When this revenue is pledged (hypothecated) to finance the infrastructure development, investment is funded by its beneficiaries – what Fred Harrison refers to as 'self-funding transport systems'.

In a stewardship economy everyone who benefits from transport infrastructure pays for the benefits they receive, whether this is as a traveller, a local business or a homeowner. Travellers pay fares and stewards whose locations benefit from the infrastructure, such as homes and businesses close to stations and transport intersections, pay higher stewardship fees.

Economists do not generally like hypothecated taxes because the revenue from the tax is likely to be either too little for the purpose identified, leading to underfunding, or too much, leading to wasteful spending. But hypothecation of stewardship fees to provide self-funding infrastructure provides the right amount of revenue – the amount that the infrastructure actually generates.

Summary

In a stewardship economy transport infrastructure is funded not by taxes on the whole population but by charges paid by those who directly benefit from it, passengers and stewards of the land that is more desirable because of the transport provision. Infrastructure provision is effective because it is self-funding and is not held back by the imposition of deadweight losses on the economy. It is fair because stewards of the land, not taxpayers as a whole, benefit from the infrastructure and contribute to its cost.

Chapter 7   Funding public services (other than transport)

In both ownership and stewardship economies the state needs to correct market failures and ensure the provision of public goods. During the 20th century public goods were increasingly funded and provided by the state until the 1980s neoliberal reforms which argued that monopoly state provision was inherently inefficient. Privatisation and the New Public Management either turned public services over to the private sector or implemented a pseudo-market based on a purchaser-provider split. The debate about the relative cost, quality and fragmentation of privately provided services will continue and this chapter focuses on the funding rather than the provision of services.

In an ownership economy, government investment in public goods requires conventional taxation with its deadweight loss.   In a stewardship economy public services can be funded without damaging to the economy. A possible funding mechanism for many public goods is the one that underpins self-funding transport infrastructure – hypothecation of stewardship fees for investment when a public good is expected to bring benefits that are reflected in rising land values.   Universal Income helps overcome market failures in a stewardship economy.

The chapter explores how education, health and social care, law and order, and the arts are currently funded and how the state might contribute to their funding in a stewardship economy.

Ownership economy

This chapter is divided into the same sort of 'silos' that characterise the government – education and training, law and order, health and social care, the arts, utilities. But the public good is an indivisible whole.   An education system is not properly contributing to the public good if it fails to provide nutritious meals for our children; a health care system is not properly contributing to the public good unless it plays its part in mitigating climate change. This is one of the main reasons why dividing up public services and putting each part out to tender separately can lead to such fragmentation that the resulting mix of services cannot achieve the overall aim.

Different governments will fund different levels of activity in public services, and in ownership economies this means different levels of taxation.

Education and training

Education may be seen as an end in itself, and training is an essential aspect of life and work. Both are required before a person enters the labour market and - particularly given the current pace of technological development - throughout their working life.

Those who think that the beneficiaries of education and training are the individuals who receive it will probably believe that people should pay for their own education. Those who think that society needs educated people and trained workers, and that a shared experience of education for the whole population leads to social solidarity will probably favour state funding.

Well-conceived and well-funded education for all at primary and secondary levels is beneficial to both individuals and to society. In the absence of public funding, it is only the already wealthy who have the resources to educate their children well, adding to inequalities and depriving the country of potentially skilled workers and educated citizens.

Graduates are more likely to be employed than non-graduates, and to earn higher salaries, which might suggest tertiary education is a private good and that university students should pay for their education themselves. On the other hand, graduates ultimately contribute more to a country's economy than non-graduates, which might suggest that they warrant some sort of subsidy.

The present arrangements for funding university education in England are deeply unsatisfactory. Universities charge tuition fees but these are less than the full cost of tuition, so providers are operating in a quasi-market. All students are eligible for loans, which allow them to fund their own studies. Students from poorer families are eligible for means-tested grants.

These arrangements have several consequences. Students who have parents wealthy enough to provide some of the finance find it easier to enter and remain in higher education.

Students, particularly those from poorer backgrounds, take on paid work during term time which interferes with their education

(Economist 30/10/99:38). They can't be expected to fulfil their potential if they have to meet their own costs of tertiary education. Even those who complete higher education are beginning their search for work saddled with debt which contributes to their difficulty in finding a deposit for a home.

Workers in ownership economies may find themselves unable to undertake training, update their skill or retrain when they need to. This may be through fear of not being able to find a job to come back to, loss of earnings while training or loss of pension rights.

Law and order

The criminal justice system is an essential part of the maintenance of a functioning society. When law and order break down we lose the benefits of co-operation and land values fall. The criminal justice system serves several, often conflicting, purposes:

Protection – where people are put in danger and there is a risk of re-offending, a case can be made for a response to crime that is focused on protecting the public. This may take the form of incarceration or surveillance.

Deterrence – knowing that you will be punished may reduce the likelihood of committing a crime. The available evidence, for many types of crime, is that people are less likely to offend if the chance of being caught is high. The connection with the type or severity of punishment is tenuous.

Rehabilitation – the offender, society and perhaps the victim would all benefit if the offender underwent personal change that made them less likely to reoffend.

Retribution – making the criminal pay for their crime can be seen as a way to reduce the unfairness of the criminal act to the victim.

The overall aim must surely be to reduce the amount of crime.

Health and social care

The funding and provision of health care and social care have evolved separately in the UK with the result that charging and financial eligibility structures are very different. However, lack of availability of social care for vulnerable people (help with bathing, preparing a meal) puts pressure on health care services. This section considers the funding of both health and social care taken together.

The provision of health and social care is important in its own right but it also underpins the whole economy. The amount of time people take off work due to sickness has a major impact on business, and availability of health care is a significant factor influencing the length of sick leave.

In the UK a firm may choose to offer private health insurance as part of its package of employee benefits, but this is very much an optional extra. In countries like the USA, health care is one of the critical aspects of employee remuneration, and otherwise profitable firms have been driven to bankruptcy by their long-term liabilities for funding health care as well as pensions.

Health and social care is expensive. Costs are unpredictable in amount and timing. There are three strategies for coping with uncertain costs. *Self-insurance* where individuals bear the risk themselves and put aside savings, where possible, to provide for future illness or dependency. *Risk-assessment* is the approach taken by commercial health insurance. The individual's health care costs are met from the premiums paid by all the insured. Just as with house, car or life insurance, the key skill of the underwriter is to assess the risk posed by each applicant and to tailor the premium, or the conditions of acceptance, accordingly. This approach means that individuals at low risk will obtain cover at relatively low rates, while those with established conditions or risk factors find it expensive, or even impossible, to obtain full cover. This discriminates against people with health problems and becomes even more problematic as predictors of longevity become more accurate, for example through genetic testing.

Risk-sharing is the approach taken by the National Health Service, where all individuals are covered and health care costs are met from general taxation. Any such system will be expensive to run because it chooses not to exclude those individuals whose genetic predisposition or current state of health mean that they would likely be ineligible for cover in self-insurance or risk-assessment based approaches. But it also creates a sense of social solidarity, a sense that 'we are all in this together', which forms an important part of our national identity.

The health and social care delivery systems of countries all over the world face a crisis in funding, whatever the source of funding and whatever mechanism they use to administer the system. The reasons include demographic change and technological developments which create an almost limitless range of possible interventions.

Arts

Lewis Hyde's magnificent exploration of the making of art in The Gift (1979/2006) suggests that what we recognise as art has its origin in the artist's desire to express their gift or talent. There are, by contrast, many examples of painting, design, writing and music that are clearly intended as commodities to be sold in the market. In making their work, an artist may receive another gift – the sense of inspiration or grace that many artists describe as flowing through them in the process of creation. In turn the work is communicated to an audience who may have the capacity to receive it as a gift.

This whole process provides an example of a gift economy, in which transactions are differ from those in a market. We may pay to visit a gallery, listen to a concert or acquire a painting, but this market exchange is quite separate from receiving the gift of the artist's work.

Lewis Hyde asked how an artist can nourish themself in a society dominated by the purchase and sale of commodities while expressing their gift in their work (Lewis Hyde 1979/2006:xvi). In a gift economy a gift (or an equivalent or greater gift) is always passed on and never hoarded. Hyde identifies three ways in which artists have resolved the question of how to support themselves – by taking a second job, by finding a patron (which might be the church, the state, a corporation or an individual) or by selling their work in the market (Lewis Hyde 1979/2006:278). Each of these enables the artist to create a protected gift-sphere in which to work.

There is a risk that, if an artist produces work in order to satisfy the market or a demanding patron, commercialisation may destroy the art. Lewis Hyde's starting point was a belief that art needs to be isolated from the market in order to protect it, but he came to accept that what is created as a gift can be sold in the market. What matters is that an artist is able to express their gift in the gift-sphere and, once it has been expressed, find out whether it has a market value (i.e., price) in the world of markets and patronage.

His favoured way for society to support the arts is by collecting some of the revenue from intellectual property rights and using this to subsidise current creative work and live performance (Lewis Hyde 1979/2006:295).

Stewardship economy

In a stewardship economy, market failures would be substantially reduced by provision of a Universal Income. Public goods could be funded from the increase in land values that they create. In a socialist version of stewardship, we all benefit from the wealth of the natural world in kind rather than in cash.

Education and training

In a stewardship economy every child, young person and adult receives a Universal Income. Provided this is sufficiently generous, as it is in a libertarian version of stewardship, individuals can contribute to the fees for their own primary, secondary and tertiary education and training.

Socialist and liberal versions of a stewardship economy may choose to invest in education from their government budget because they see it as a public good in its own right, or because they can justify it as an investment that stimulates the economy and so generates revenue through increased stewardship fees.

When choosing where to live, parents take account of local schools. When secondary school heads discuss the sort of indicators by which they would like to be assessed, they sometimes propose using house prices in their catchment areas, which are known to rise after a favourable Ofsted report (Economist 14/4/2001). In the example of Reading, where pupils were assigned to schools quite strictly by catchment area, it was calculated that if an average house could have been moved from the catchment area of the primary school with the poorest results at Key Stage 2 to that of the primary school with the best results at this stage it would increase in price by over 33 per cent (Cheshire & Sheppard 2004). McClay and Harrison (2004) studied this effect in Christchurch, New Zealand and found an increase in house prices relative to the sample mean price of 48 per cent for the best girls' secondary school and 28 per cent for the best boys' school with this uplift for the best girls' school being similar to the fees of a comparable private school.

A case can be made for the revenue from the higher stewardship fees of family homes in the catchment areas of desirable schools to be used to fund increased investment in education. Some would favour rewarding the successful schools, some the less successful and some would favour increased funding for all schools equally, depending on their political persuasion.

Universal Income contributes significantly to covering the costs of university education and paying for programmes of training and re-training.

Law and order

The criminal justice system is funded by the state in any version of stewardship as it is clearly a guardian function. But land values are lower in areas where there is a lot of street crime and vandalism, so investment in crime reduction could be self-financing if it led to an increase in revenue from stewardship fees.

Universal Income offers new ways of thinking about punishment as deductions could be made from an individual's Universal Income. If incarceration is required, the person's Universal Income might be used to contribute to meeting its costs. When retribution or deterrence is required it might be appropriate to 'fine' the offender some proportion of their Universal Income. Of course, fines are already widely used in ownership economies. But 25 per cent of the prison population in the UK are incarcerated for non-payment of fines, which would not happen if the financial penalty was deducted at source. Such fines might improve the probability of rehabilitation simply by keeping people out of prison. Any suggestion of the withdrawal of Universal Income has to be considered very carefully, as non-withdrawability is such a central plank of the very similar Citizens' Income.

Health and social care

A libertarian version of stewardship provides the highest levels of Universal Income, with little direct expenditure by the state. It would require the individual to fund their own health and social care through a combination of self-insurance and commercial insurance. A liberal version might rely on commercial insurance but would try to limit the discrimination against high-risk individuals that is required by rational underwriters.

A socialist version of stewardship provides some form of risk-sharing through government funding of the health and social care delivery system. The health and social care could be provided either by the state or by independent providers from the for-profit or the not-for-profit sectors. However, the great dangers of privatising provision are the fragmentation of the service, escalating administrative costs and risk of provider failure with serious consequences for those receiving services.

Arts

The arts are an example of a public good, and of a gift economy, that receive some automatic support in a stewardship economy because everyone, including artists, receives a small private income in the form of a Universal Income. That might not be sufficient, but it provides a significant platform to support artistic work. We can think of the Universal Income as a mechanism for recycling the gift wealth of the natural world as a gift to every person and those who use this to support their artistic work would then be recycling the gift wealth and using it to make their own gifts.

Utilities

In the same way that transport can be self-financing, if increases in land value are captured and used to fund transport provision, so the provision of other sorts of infrastructure like the utilities could tap in to the increase in land values that these produce.

Benefit-cost calculations and investment decisions, similar to those for transport infrastructure, must be made for the utilities. For many utilities, the so-called natural monopolies, it makes no sense to duplicate the provision of infrastructure for electricity, water, gas and sewage. The telephone network used to be a natural monopoly but is now subject to competition from mobile phone networks. Investment decisions for telecoms are most appropriately left to the private sector, within a regulatory framework.

In a stewardship economy each of the natural monopolies is held in Trust by a stewardship trust and is subject to a regulatory body in very much the same way as transport networks. The stewardship trust allocates franchises to the highest bidder. If the utility companies anticipate that they can operate at a profit they bid to make a payment. If they anticipate that they will run at a loss, they bid for a subsidy.

In the same way as with transport infrastructure, an operating or investment subsidy for utilities infrastructure projects is made available only if a business case can be made that this infrastructure will sufficiently increase the stewardship fees paid by the plots of land affected. This ensures that all infrastructure is self-funding.

Summary

The financing of public services from general taxation presents a major challenge to governments in an ownership economy because taxes fall on income and profits and cause a deadweight loss to the economy. We need to find ways of funding public goods, and of recognising this spending as investment rather than as a drain on the exchequer. The increase in economic activity and land values resulting from improved education and training, law and order and health could be used to fund this investment.

The purpose of stewardship is to use the gift of the natural world for the benefit of all. Investing in public goods is probably a vitally important way of using this revenue.

A stewardship economy could choose to treat health and social care as a public good funded from the government budget, or as a private good that people are enabled to purchase by their Universal Income. Universal Income provides financial support for people undergoing education and training and an element of self-funding could be introduced into education by tapping into the impact that educational institutions have on local property values. Deductions from the Universal Income provide an alternative to cash fines, and this would reduce the prison population. And the Universal Income supports creative and voluntary work in the gift economy.